FREDERICK BARBER

Lifescapes

Find Your Place ... Live Your Dream (And Profit in the Process)

PLATYPUS
PUBLISHING

First published by Platypus Publishing 2023

First edition

This book was professionally typeset on Reedsy.
Find out more at reedsy.com

Contents

I

The Problem

Our contemporary world is not designed to lead to happy, healthy lives. We operate out of assumptions as to where and how we should live that do not make sense in a world of remote work, geographically dispersed families, and the need to create real community. There has to be, and there is, a better way.

1

There's Gotta Be a Better Way (Spoiler Alert: I'm going to show you one...)

Throughout my adult life, I operated under a basic premise of how the course of my career and later life should play out. After college, I identified a career path and location where I would establish myself. This path took a few turns, from a first job and grad school in Washington, DC, a few years working overseas, 8 years in Austin, Texas and then a career move to Dallas in 2005. The basic premise of this life model said to buy a nice house in a suburban community of a major metropolitan area with good schools. So that's what we did - in the Steiner Ranch neighborhood of Austin, and then in rapidly-growing Frisco, Texas. Both were great places to raise our kids. Our financial planner encouraged us to pay it off in no more than 15 years, while also piling money into 401(k) and 529 plans for the kid's education.

Once we became empty-nesters (which for my wife and I happened in 2020), we had a few choices:

We could stay where we are, "aging in place" in a paid off home. Our home would be a gathering place for the extended family for as long as it makes sense. The house would represent a secure financial asset. Once paid off, it would be inexpensive to live in, while continuing to grow in value year after year. Of course, our health might deteriorate, or our children may no longer be interested in returning to their home town, necessitating a change in the future.

Or, after retiring, we could move to Florida, Arizona or some other place with a nice climate and good recreational options, where we would settle in with others in our age group, cruising around in a golf cart and playing Bridge at the club.

Ideally, whichever choice we make, we'd have the ability to travel and otherwise enjoy the fruits of our labor and the secure financial foundation we have built. But regardless of the specific course of action, the process was essentially linear: after college, get a job, buy a home, stay there a long time while you raise a family, then determine where you want to be as you grow old.

But as my career transformed over the course of the Covid-19 pandemic, moving to a distributed, remote workforce for my company, and as our three adult children found their lives pulled to other, far-away metropolitan areas, I began to wonder: does this model still make sense? Is there a solution that would be better suited to our longer-term needs, perhaps even more financially rewarding, and frankly more fun. Let's be honest, once the kids are grown, and particularly if they don't settle down in the same town as you, the suburbs can be kind of boring. Few suburban neighborhoods offer much that you can walk to, so life revolves around getting in the car to go somewhere. The most attractive natural landscapes might be a lake by a town park, or maybe just the landscaping around a shopping center.

Our contemporary culture suffers from two major crises that

affect a wide array of people: an epidemic of loneliness, and a sedentary lifestyle. I would argue that the contemporary suburban career and residential model makes both of these worse. We have engineered a lifestyle that is intrinsically bad for us.

We live in communities that are designed for isolation. Many people can't tell you the names of their neighbors, let alone any pertinent facts about them. Oftentimes, our social relationships are built around contexts such as our children's schools, sports or other extracurricular activities. Once those contexts change, the relationships end. Most middle-aged people count the number of friends with whom they routinely interact in the single digits. As I will discuss in greater detail later in this book, the leading theorists in healthy aging now argue that "aging in place" can be one of the worst choices we can make. Place, in fact, is often the problem.

A choice of place also leads in many cases to a sedentary lifestyle. If we don't have options to walk to any meaningful destinations — be it a coffee shop, a grocery store, a place of worship, a sports facility, or a gathering place for friends, we either jump in a car or stay home on the sofa. Dr. James Levine, an endocrinologist at the Mayo Clinic, coined an apt phrase: "Sitting is the new smoking". An article in the cardiology journal *Circulation* concluded that "no amount of physical activity is enough to combat the dangerous health effects of sitting for hours each day." Researchers at UCLA have shown that prolonged periods of sitting are associated with thinning of the medial temporal lobe, an area of the brain that plays a role in making memories. So a sedentary lifestyle can actually contribute to dementia. Our sedentary suburban life is fueling a crisis of public health that is leading to disease and reduced life expectancy.

But stuck in the suburbs, what are we supposed to do about it? It is simply a fact in many communities that getting in our recommended 10,000 steps per day becomes a task, rather than a natural outcome from living our normal lives. A while ago I visited with an old friend who had left a job in Silicon Valley where he had a 75 minute one-way commute for a new role in Ann Arbor, Michigan (in an equally attractive technology company). His new home is walking distance from the University of Michigan football stadium and an array of shops, coffee joints and produce markets. He and his wife walk everywhere, and he now puts less than 7,500 miles per year on his car. The benefits to his health, including his mental well-being, have been tremendous.

Looking at these trends and seeing the adverse effects, I began to formulate concepts for what could be a better way. The Covid-19 pandemic accelerated trends that had been percolating for a long-time in the Western world: distributed, remote work, performed from flexible locations. Putting these trends together forms the basis of what I call a "Lifescape": a design for a living context that combines Place, People, Purpose, Pleasure and the Potential for Profit in an environment that is healthier, more engaging, and more fun. And best of all, we don't need to wait until we retire to create our ideal Lifescape! In fact, while I am writing primarily to an audience of people in the empty-nester, pre-retired life stage (where I can speak from personal experience), many of the ideas in this book can be applied to people at any stage of life.

As you read this book, you will discover how to create your own personal Lifescape.

You will explore how you can identify the place that works best for you at this and future stages of your life. You will work through a quantitative and qualitative assessment of what constitutes the right location and residential options that can help you to live a better quality of life, maximizing the benefits of your financial resources, while not becoming "house poor." Your choice of place will have as a central principle the idea of being walkable and cultivating a lifestyle that gets you off the sofa and out in the streets and trails of the place you call home.

Very importantly, you will see that place need not be just one location. In fact, "places" might be a better term. We will go through examples of how a mobile lifestyle, combining one or more physical homes with nomadic options (with an RV, short-term rentals, or other work-travel concepts) can maximize the potential of places to fit your life goals.

You will develop effective strategies for ensuring that you have people in your life that you can relate to in meaningful, healthy and fun ways. Our modern world does not make this as natural or easy as it once was. But there are proven methods that can help to overcome the epidemic of loneliness and ensure that you are arranging your life circumstances in ways that create natural groupings of people, where real connections can be built.

You will re-examine the assumptions of the financial model for long-term security. We will look critically at the idea of building equity in a primary residence as the cornerstone of your financial plan. Millions of Americans have significant wealth concentrated in their homes as a result of the run-up in values that has taken place since 2000. Similar trends exist in many other countries as well. The question becomes how much is too much, and is a single primary residence the best place to store that wealth. I will show you how you can downsize, free up capital for other uses, and even use your residence to generate income while you travel for part of the year.

In addition to examining the trends and providing examples of alternative models for your redesigned life, you will have access to the custom Lifescapes tool, a proprietary software system available at LifeScapes.info, to help you build your own plan.

****

So why am I the guy to show you a better way?

I am not a psychologist or an expert in personal well-being. I am not a real estate or financial professional. But I do bring a lot of expertise to the task. I am a quantitative social scientist. After majoring in Sociology at Cornell, I started my career with *American Demographics*, a Dow Jones publication, where I researched and wrote on social and behavioral trends. I have a Masters degree in Applied Demography (from Georgetown University) and a 35 year career in consulting, advertising and market research, working with leading companies and organizations on adapting to changes in society and consumer behavior. I spent 10 years as the Chief Analytics Officer of a major media company, and a I now run a market research technology firm. In short, I'm really good at making sense of data and understanding trends. My wife is a CPA, and I've leaned on her in certain parts of this book to provide analysis of the tax and financial implications of some of the strategies I suggest. And most importantly, I am able to describe a life design process that my wife and I are currently living through, where we have explored these same questions and developed answers that we feel can be informative to others. We have done our best to base the ideas in this book on the available data and foresight into emerging trends. These strategies have worked for us, and I believe that they will work for you, too.

But first, let me tell you a story that started me down this path...

2

A Walk in the Park

It was a nice Saturday in the Fall, and my friend Tom and I decided to head out to a nearby town park in the northern suburbs of Dallas to hike along the shore of Lake Lewisville and catch up on life.

Along with the typical pavilions and a boat ramp, this park had a small area for RVs - about 50 spaces under the trees on a peninsula jutting out into the lake. I thought it would be fun to see what kind of rigs were camping there that weekend, while lecturing Tom on the merits of a Class A, a 5th wheel or a classic Airstream. So we headed over to the RV section of the park.

My wife and I had purchased a 29' travel trailer earlier that year and had taken a few trips to get out of the Texas heat. We drove up to Ruidoso, New Mexico over Labor Day, and then in October to Arches and Zion National Parks in Utah. These were "work-cations" for me. Running the U.S. division of a small European tech company, disappearing into the wild, *a la* Nomadland, is not an option for me. But I could work from a campsite as long as I had access to the internet, and in the afternoons we could head out on a hike or walk to a cool brewpub.

My wife and I were starting to think about how this could be a more routine part of our lives, hoping to figure out a way to spend a few months of the year away from home. We had recently become empty-nesters, and my company had moved to a fully remote work environment during the Covid-19 pandemic. So there was really nothing keeping us in Dallas. But there were some niggling problems with our plan: the house always needed some attention, between caring for the lawn and pool or attending to routine maintenance and housekeeping issues. And while we were away, the costs continued. The heat and air conditioning, homeowners insurance, etc. did not stop if we chose to spend a month on the road. It just didn't seem practical to do more than the occasional long weekend or slightly longer "work-cation" or pleasure trip.

But then things got interesting.

Walking through the RV park, we struck up a conversation with three couples who were gathered around a big screen TV mounted on the side of a 40' 5th wheel watching college football and sipping margaritas. These couples, who each had an RV parked on an adjacent site of this scenic lakeside peninsula, we learned had all sold their houses during the pandemic and were living full-time in their campers. They traveled from park to park around the Dallas/Fort Worth Metroplex, all while continuing to work in their careers. One was a CPA with a Ft. Worth firm. Another was a commercial construction manager. The third was an insurance loss adjuster. They had all made the decision to move out of their houses independently, had met through serendipity at various campsites, and now for the most part traveled together, spending 2-4 weeks at a time in a different location. (Most public campsites will only let you stay a set maximum number of days at a time, so they typically had to hook up and move every 15-20 days).

The CPA, a women in her early 50s, talked through the advantages:

> *We were paying over $10,000 a year in property taxes, and a similar amount for maintenance, plus utilities. And the value of the house had gone up significantly. We chose to free up that equity and simplify our lifestyle, putting a little bit of the proceeds into the camper and truck, while investing the bulk of our home equity in a balanced set of ETFs that will compound in value as much as, or more, than our house had done. Our cost of living is dramatically reduced, and our quality of life is greatly improved. We have so much less to stress about. Sometimes at work people ask where I live and I joke that I'm sleeping in a van down by the river! But the reality is so much better. We are enjoying some of the most beautiful places in the area, with nature literally outside our door. We have all the space and all the "toys" we need. And we have freed up thousands of dollars a month in our budget. I don't know why we would ever want to go back to a sticks-and-bricks house!*

I was intrigued. Here was a sub-culture I never knew existed, who had made some radical adjustments in their living conditions, and appeared to be thriving. I wondered, "is this for real? Can it make sense - both personally and financially?" And are there other options that could make this even more generalizable? — since living in an RV isn't for everyone.

The Covid-19 pandemic radically changed the nature of work for millions of people, allowing workplace norms to catch up with what technology has made possible. The three couples I met had a variety of reasons to stay close to home in the DFW area, but for others, it might be possible to live in a few different places and to migrate to where the weather is great, the food terrific, and family and friends beckon. I have always enjoyed a beautiful landscape, be it a rugged natural setting where it seems God has placed everything in perfect alignment, or a fine English garden that has been meticulously arranged to provide a postcard view at every turn. So as I thought of the goal in front of us, a term came to mind: "Lifescapes" — applying these design principles to the parameters of place, people, purpose and pleasure with the potential for profit, so that we live where we want to, work where we enjoy it, and flourish in the process.

Join me as we go on the Lifescape adventure together!

3

Reality 2023

There is said to be an old Chinese curse: "may you live in interesting times."

(Fun fact: The actual Chinese proverb, roughly translated, is "Better to be a dog in times of tranquility than a human in times of chaos").

But we do live in a very interesting time, with a few curses, and a lot of blessings. Take a look at these data:

- The run-up of housing values in the past several years has generated significant paper profits for home owners. From 2019 through 2022, median home values in the United States increased by over 17% each year.[1] Similar trends were seen in many other countries as well, in particular Canada, the UK, Europe and Australia. This is a blessing and a curse, in that while this unrealized capital gain represents significant net worth for millions of homeowners, it comes with the added burden of increased property taxes and difficulty in finding less expensive housing options.

- The share of jobs worked remotely has increased five-fold since 2019. The Census Bureau's Household Pulse Survey reports that in 2023, 26% of the workforce — around 25 million people — work entirely from home. This rate was obviously higher at the peak of the Covid-19 pandemic, peaking at over 65% in May, 2020.[2] But nonetheless, this represents a significant shift in the structure of the workforce. Prior to the pandemic, less than 5% of Americans worked from home.[3]

In terms of attitudes towards remote work, consider the following:

- 67% feel the greatest benefit of remote work is flexibility in how they spend their time.
- 31% of US employers exclusively hire remote workers.
- 62% of workers feel more productive when working remotely.
- 74% of professionals believe remote work will become the new normal.[4]

Technology has enabled this transformation. In 2020, the U.S. Census Bureau estimated that 93.8% of households have broadband internet access. Gigabit-speed internet services, once a rarity, are now found in many smaller cities, ranging from Natchez, MS, to Charleston, WV, Terre Haute, IN, Cumberland, MD, Elmira, NY and Roswell, NM. With nationwide 5G services increasingly available, the ability to access cloud-based services at blazingly-fast speeds is becoming widespread across the US and abroad. On the T-Mobile network, I get 5G download speeds of over 300Mbps on my 2 acre property 30 miles outside of Dallas, TX. In more remote areas, Starlink provides up to 200Mbps download speeds anywhere with a clear view of the sky.

Companies have embraced this new technology. The usage of Microsoft Teams, for example, nearly doubled between 2021 and 2022, from 145 million to 270 million users. Over one million organizations use Microsoft Teams as their default messaging platform[5], including 91 of the 100 largest US corporations.[6] Other cloud-based workplace collaboration platforms, from companies like Google, Slack, Atlassian and Teamwork round out this market. In short, there are very few organizations that do not enable at least some degree of remote work today, and very few employees who are not able to avail themselves of the possibility.

The run-up in home values has impacted some areas more than others, but is nonetheless widespread. According to data from Zillow, home prices in the U.S. have climbed over 42 percent between 2010 and 2020, with this rate of increase accelerating even more during the Covid-19 pandemic. As more and more people worked from home, people were willing to pay more for the home they wanted. Coupled with historically low interest rates over the past decade, this created a perfect storm for home value appreciation. Zillow data shows that several cities in California saw home prices more than double between 2010 and 2020, and many cities in Florida, Arizona and Texas experienced nearly as large run-ups in home values.

There is a correlation between median household income and the percentage change in home price, meaning that home prices have grown more rapidly in more affluent areas. I was born in Buffalo, NY, a city where the average home value has barely budged. But even in that market, homes in the historical Allentown neighborhood, and in affluent suburbs like Williamsville (my childhood hometown), Clarence and East Aurora have seen double-digit value increases. Of course, moves by central banks to raise interest rates to combat inflation after 2021 have taken much of the wind out of these sails, and home prices have begun to decline slightly in some markets. But this does not negate the longer-term trend that has created significant unrealized gains for many homeowners over the past decade.

As of 2022, the average home owner in the United States is sitting on $185,000 in home equity.[7] This average number increased by almost $48,000 in 2021 alone! Cumulatively, US homeowners have unrealized gains over of $23 trillion, according to Federal Reserve data. 42% of homeowners have paid off more than half of the value of their home. In 2018, Trulia calculated that over 3 million homes in America were worth more than $1 million. Just four years later, in 2022, the number had doubled to 6 million homes, according to Redfin. In markets like San Francisco and San Jose, this is the norm, with more than 85% of homes valued at more than $1 million. But even places like Mt Pleasant, SC, Missoula, MT and Salt Lake City, UT have seen significant growth in the share of million-dollar-plus homes.[8]

If $185,000 is the average home equity, that means that, by definition, half of home owners have more than that amount — and many have much more. In 2020, roughly 15.3 million households – about 12% of American households – had a net worth, including the value of their primary residence, in excess of $1 million.

But as we will explore in more detail in the next chapter, concentrating a significant share of wealth in a primary residence may not be the best strategy. While the run-up of home values in recent years may seem like a party that will never stop, at some point it will. And that point may already be here. Home price forecasts for 2023 show little prospect for growth. Some sources predict 0% growth or decline in the national median home price, while others expect a modest increase of 3%-6%. Some markets, especially the most expensive ones, may see a significant drop of 5% to 10% this year.

Historically, home prices have only increased 3-4% per year, barely keeping pace with inflation. So while a house has represented a safe store of wealth, while of course also providing obvious benefits beyond the purely financial return, it may not be the best investment. Looking at our own financial situation, we found ourselves sitting on way more equity than made sense, and way more house than we needed as well once the kids had moved out. We had reached an inflection point — where the rate of growth in value was decreasing and looked less likely to keep up with inflation. It was time to realize some of that gain and re-allocate resources. Millions of Americans are reaching the same conclusion, cashing out of their suburban McMansions for a more sustainable living arrangement.

Another crucial inflection point has been reached in the area of health. For decades, Americans, along with most of the developed world, saw rapidly increasing life expectancy and the promise of decades of healthy living post-retirement. In his book *Replace Retirement*, author John Anderson painted a rosy picture of an "exponential" future for the Baby Boom generation, where living healthily to 100 and beyond would become the new norm. He based this projection on trends in the post-World War II era, where life expectancy had increased from

68 years in 1950 (barely 3 years past retirement!) to 79 years by 2013. But then something strange happened. The improvement stopped. Between 2013 and 2023, life expectancy in the US did not budge. It remains right at 79 years.[9] By 2030, only a modest increase is expected, to around 80 years. This is not an anomaly due to premature deaths from Covid-19. The trend had begun well before the pandemic, and while there was a noticeable "blip" in the death rate data for 2020 and 2021, this does not explain the plateauing of life expectancy.

While significant improvements have occurred in our ability to treat many diseases, particularly cancers, other disease rates are increasing. From 2001 to 2020, cancer death rates went down 27%, according to the U.S. Centers for Disease Control and Prevention. Importantly, the biggest drop is found for lung cancer deaths, and this can largely be attributed to the reduced rates of smoking in the U.S. in the decades prior. The same data from the CDC shows that deaths from heart disease in the U.S. have actually *increased* by over 4% per year over the past few years, reversing a decade of improvement. And from 2001 to 2020, the share of Americans with diabetes *significantly* increased. So while we can be proud of the huge improvements that have been made in battling cancer, a disease that often killed people quickly, the news is not so good with regard to heart disease and diabetes, which tend to kill people more slowly. As we discussed briefly at the beginning of this book, the increasing prevalence of heart disease and diabetes are strongly related to our increasingly sedentary lifestyle. And it could in fact be killing us.

A study published at the end of 2017 in the *Annals of Internal Medicine* found evidence that sitting for long periods of time is a risk factor for early death. People who sit the most, when compared to those who sat the least, had an increase in disease and death, specifically:

- Their diabetes risk increased by 112 percent.
- They had a 147 percent increase in cardiovascular events, like heart attacks and strokes.
- They had a 90 percent increase in death from cardiovascular events.
- They had a 49 percent increase in death from any cause.

So, what can we conclude from these trends:

1. Millions of people are sitting in homes with way more equity than they need.
2. The key word in the sentence above is "sitting." Engineered into a sedentary suburban lifestyle, we are undermining our long-term health, as already evidenced by the trends.
3. But we don't need to live this way. Technology has enabled us to live and work anywhere, and increasingly employers are more than willing to go along with this desire.

As we explore how to make changes to improve our health, wealth, and overall well being, let's next take a look at the true cost of home ownership.

4

The True Cost of Home Ownership

My wife and I have made a few good financial moves in our lives. Our ability to identify nice places to live and buy a home before the local market took off has certainly been one of them. I don't consider myself some sort of a real estate genius; for the most part, we were just lucky. But the fact is, we, like millions of other Americans, have made good money on our homes.

After a four year stint in the 90s living and working overseas, we decided to move to Austin, Texas. We didn't know many people in Austin - it just seemed like a cool place to live. We had just had our first child, and settling down in the Washington, DC area, where we had met and where my wife had grown up, just didn't seem to fit the mold for the family life we were hoping to create. In Austin in 1997, it was possible to buy a house in a nice neighborhood for around $200,000, and be able to afford it on my income alone as Alice focused on raising our daughter (and two other children who came along in the next few years).

We bought a new construction home in the rapidly growing Steiner Ranch neighborhood near Lake Travis, west of Austin.

We lived there until 2005, when a career opportunity led us to move to Dallas. We made a nice profit at the time. Today, that house is valued at well over $600,000. In Dallas, we moved into the suburb of Frisco, which over the next decade was routinely listed as one of the fastest growing cities in America. Frisco had two high schools when we moved there. Today is has 12 (and probably more by the time you are reading this). We lived in two houses in Frisco over the next decade, and made a nice profit on each. We then moved across the Metroplex to a more rural area, where we built a custom home on two acres. That house has appreciated by over $1 million since we built it in 2015.

We have worked with a great financial planner for the past 15 years. One of his core pieces of advice was to stay within a 15 year mortgage and aim to have the house paid off before we retire, to enable "rent free" living as we age in place.

Sounds like great advice, right? For some people, it might be. But, as I will explain, for many people, staying in the house you raised your family in, even if it is paid in full, might be entirely the wrong thing to do. There are several reasons for this. As discussed in the previous chapter, an appreciated home may be located in a sedentary and isolated suburban environment, which no longer serves your needs once the priorities of schools and kid's activities are no longer your reason for being in that place. The context for location changes, and remaining in that place can lead to stagnation and decline in physical and psychological health. We will discuss this in detail in the next chapter.

For now, let's take a look at what it really costs to live in your primary residence, even one that is "paid off."

As we all know, you never really can live rent free. The privilege of living in any city, town or village comes with an array of costs. Someone has to pay for those great schools, to fix the potholes in the roads, for the police, the fire department and the local parks. That property tax bill keeps on coming every year. In Texas, where we laud the fact that we don't pay any State income tax, the bills get paid largely through property tax. Our statewide average property tax rate is 1.8% of the value of the home per year. Only a handful of States charge more: Connecticut (2.14%), Illinois (2.27%), New Hampshire (2.18%), New Jersey (2.49%), Vermont (1.9%), and Wisconsin (1.86%).[10] California has a low property tax rate, averaging 0.76%, but the much higher average value of homes in that State leads to a very high annual dollar amount paid in property tax — unless you bought the house years ago and are protected from property tax increases by Proposition 13. Of course, this rate can vary from town to town depending on the local school tax and other factors. In my County in Texas, property taxes average 2.14%. Let's use 2% as an average figure for a "high property tax" State. On a $500,000 home, that's $10,000/year. On a $1 million dollar home, it's $20,000. My own property tax on a 5,600 square foot custom home on 2 acres was well above that $20,000 figure.

And then of course there is the cost of water, heat and electricity. Americans spend a monthly average of $429.33 per month on utilities. Annually, this is an average cost of $5,151.99, according to the Consumer Expenditure Survey by the U.S. Bureau of Labor Statistics. And of course 50% of homeowners spend more than the average. My monthly utility bills easily ran twice this amount. So, let's call it, on average, $10,000/year on a large suburban family home. Now we're up to $30,000/year for property tax and utilities.

Then we need to factor in upkeep. While some items vary widely from year to year, like the cost of a new roof or replacing an HVAC system, it seems reasonable to budget another $5,000 for stuff that breaks. On top of that there is the cost of lawn care, pool maintenance if you live in one, HOA fees. It's not hard for that all to add up to $5,000 more.

So, we are at $40,000/year to live in a "paid for" house valued at $500,000. It could easily be much more. But you get my point. A $500,000 home has an 8% annual operating cost. You are effectively paying over $3,000/month "rent" to live in a paid-for home. The math improves somewhat as the value of the home goes up, provided that the increase in utility costs and maintenance does not increase linearly with home value — but regardless of how you do the calculation, it is hard to come to a scenario where the annual operating cost is less than 5% of the value of the home. Therefore, unless the value of the home is increasing by at least that amount, you are not making money. Would you pay a 5% annual asset management fee on an asset that increased in value by less than 5% per year?

A financial analyst would be quick to point out that my math here is incomplete. You need to also consider the cost of the alternative. Anywhere you live will have costs for property tax (either explicit, or imputed in the rent you pay), utilities, and most likely maintenance and lawn care. But if you are living in a house that is no longer appropriate for your stage of life, you may be paying much more in operating costs than you are earning in real estate appreciation. And sometimes, that value may go down. The goal is to "right-size" and "right-place" your real estate; you need to own enough home in the right type of location for healthy living, but not so much that you are foregoing financial and personal freedom. You need to look very carefully at what the home you are currently in actually costs, and ask yourself: "if I were to free up some of that equity and downsize to a more appropriate place, how much could I make on that equity if it were properly invested?"

We saw that argument being made by the CPA I met at our town park, who sold her home and now lives in 40' 5th-wheel RV. Her solution was radical, for sure. But her logic is sound, and she and her husband are having a lot of fun! Let's assume, for sake of argument, that they sold their home and cleared $250,000 in capital gain. The already owned a half ton pickup truck, and I would guess that the 5th wheel ran them in the range of $75,000. That's $175,000 that they have now invested. In a properly weighted basket of ETFs, historically they could expect to gain 8-9% per year. That's approximately $15,000 in the first year, and with compounding it will grow quickly in the years to come. Their monthly operating cost for propane, RV park fees and maintenance might run $2,000, which is probably equivalent to what they had been paying on a mortgage if their home was not paid off. Now let's assume that they had paid off their home, and walked away with a $500,000 gain. Now, after investing the net proceeds of $425,000, they will earn on average $35,000 in the first year in dividends and capital gains, versus $24,000 in monthly costs, and those earnings will compound and grow to more each year. The RV will depreciate by around 10% per year, and they will likely end up replacing it every 3-5 years. But in the meantime, they are saving thousands of dollars per month.

This is only one model for a radical change that puts the true cost of home ownership into perspective. There are countless other permutations of the model, and this book will help you to figure out what structure is right for you. But the thing I want you to walk away with is the idea that it is possible you have *too much* equity in your home, and that there are better ways to deploy the funds.

5

Place is the Problem ... and the Solution

As we have seen, living in the wrong place, or a place that has long since served its purpose, can be a problem. It can tie up funds that could grow more effectively in more liquid investments. And it can lock you into an environment that is fundamentally unhealthy. You can end up isolated from family and friends and stuck in a structure and neighborhood that does not fit the priorities for an active lifestyle as you age. But getting place right can make all the difference in the world. It can provide for lower stress, greater happiness, improved social connections and increased financial returns.

Full disclosure - my thinking on the importance of getting place right is not original. Ryan Frederick writes extensively on this topic in his book *Right Place, Right Time: The Ultimate Guide to Choosing a Home for the Second Half of Life*. A lot of my thinking about aging in place vs. finding the right place is informed by Frederick's book. Frederick has spent his life studying healthy aging and building communities that are designed for successful living in a multi-generational context. His work has been cited by Kiplinger, Forbes, CBS News and others, and is endorsed by leading experts in the field. Another person who has written extensively on the topic of social isolation is Sheila Liming, a professor at Champlain College and author of *Hanging Out: The Radical Power of Killing Time*. Her views on the "quiet catastrophe" of failing to spend time outside of our family and workplace is well summarized on the Ezra Klein Show podcast from April 2023, entitled "We've Built Our World for Loneliness. We Could Rebuild for Community." Adding to this body of knowledge, Dr. Vivek Murthy, the US Surgeon General, wrote *Together: The Healing Power of Human Connection in a Sometimes Lonely World*. Dr. Murthy has referred to loneliness as a health epidemic. In a 2017 *Harvard Business Review* article, he wrote that as a physician "the most common pathology I saw was not heart disease or diabetes; it was loneliness."[11] These are smart people, and they have done the research on the need to identify a place that is appropriate for your overall well-being as you grow older. So, I will quote liberally from them in this chapter.

In *Right Place, Right Time*, Frederick writes: "The role of place is [a] factor often overlooked in its impact on our well-being. Country, region, state, metropolitan area, neighborhood, nearby streets, and physical dwelling all play a role in our health." He cites research that shows that natural light, air quality and access to nature all impact your health, as well as the need for a structure that is designed with the appropriate elements that make for safety in a home as one ages, such as non-slip tiles in a bathroom and access to the street without stairs.

In particular, Frederick argues against the traditional notion of aging in place. Don't get me wrong; there are situations where aging in place can make sense. If you have an extensive set of family and community relationships in the place where you live, the community is walkable and safe, and the physical dwelling unit is appropriate for your current and future needs as you age, by all means, stay put.

But, as Frederick notes, in many cases "aging in place does not deliver on its promise. It is rarely the right strategy for the long term, particularly if one is looking to make the most of the benefits of a longer life." Some of the drawbacks of the aging in place model include:

- Housing that is not designed well for people to live in safely as they grow older
- Limited walkability and lack of access to any form of public transportation
- Inefficient access to services that need to come to you
- Declining economic appeal of neighborhoods that may be past their prime

And then of course there is the opportunity cost of the money that may be tied up in the home. If, for instance, you are sitting on $500,000 or more in home equity in a house that is now too big for your needs, cashing that out and living in a place that is smaller and less expensive to both own and maintain can allow hundreds of thousands of dollars to be re-directed towards investments with greater liquidity, and likely a higher rate of return. Frederick presents one example: "if someone has home equity of $300,000 in a stagnant housing market and the stock market yields a 7% return, this is an annual opportunity cost to the house owner of more than $20,000. This cost is hard to remember because there is no bill associated with it."

But the greatest risk to aging in place, beyond the physical and financial challenges outlined above, is the risk of social isolation. To quote from Frederick's book again:

> *"Simply put, a home that at one time represented comfort and connection with friends and family can become a place of solitary confinement and loneliness. Environments change in relation to our needs and abilities. What was great for a young family may be a challenge for older adults without the built-in social networks that schools and kids' activities [once provided]. Turnover in a neighborhood also affects social networks. About half of older adults don't know* any *of their current neighbors."*

As Dr. Murthy, the Surgeon General, argues, this lack of social connection is a pathological problem. A 2018 report by the Kaiser Family Foundation stated that 22% of adults said they often or always feel socially isolated. Between 1990 and 2021, the share of Americans who reported having 5 or more close friends declined by 25 percentage points. If social isolation is an epidemic, as Dr. Murthy stated, aging in place can be one of the greatest risk factors for catching this disease.

I saw this play out with my mother. I grew up in a nice suburban ranch house in Williamsville, New York, a suburb of Buffalo. My parents bought the house in 1964, a few months before I was born. My mother paid it off shortly after I graduated from college. (She and my father had divorced when I was young, and she raised my sisters and me in that home). Being a single story home in a community she knew well, she felt that she could live there for the duration, and for a while it worked well. But the drawbacks Frederick notes were apparent as she got into her 70s. The washer and dryer were in the basement, and she feared that if she ever fell going up and down the stairs, she could lay there for days before anyone would be alerted. This was not paranoia; the risk was real. My sisters and I had all moved away, and she only had a few friends left in town. All of the other houses on the street had turned over, with new young families moving in, none of whom had any connection to her. And the declining economy of that Rust Belt city did not do much for home value appreciation. Of course, there was also the snow.

She took care of her aging mother for several years until my grandmother passed away, and then we started looking at what made sense next. We sold the home that she had lived in for 42 years and purchased a 3 bedroom, one-story home next door to us in Frisco, Texas. Her new home had a pool, which my kids thoroughly enjoyed! My nephew, her grandson, moved in for a season when a job brought him to the area. As her health declined, we made another decision to sell both houses and buy a new home with a mother-in-law suite, where she could live semi-independently but also have caregivers come in to help her, without disturbing the rest of the family. By getting her out of the "aging in place" model, we established a greater social connection for her and our family, provided a safe and supportive environment, and also did better financially from the appreciation of these homes.

So what are the attributes that make a place the solution, instead of the problem? I'll focus on three:

1. Facilitating social connections, through convenient "third places" (more on that term coming up)
2. An environment that is conducive to year-round physical activity.

3. A safe place, in terms of the community at large, access to quality health care and social support services, and the physical design of the residence

Frederick writes a lot about the importance of "third places." If home is one place, and work is another, a third place is a location where community connections happen. This can be a coffee shop, a wine bar, places of worship, a park or even just a streetscape where people stop and talk to one another. For a third place to work, it needs to form a focal point in a community. It should be a place you can walk to (or maybe bike); not surrounded by a huge concrete parking lot. The people who frequent this space need to live in the area and find themselves there organically. Think of the corner pub in England. American communities are distressingly devoid of such spaces. I was amazed one day when I drove into the old town section of Coppell, Texas, about 15 miles from my home. There in the center of town was a large public green space, home to a Farmer's Market on Saturdays, with a Performing Arts Center, several restaurants, and George Coffee. George Coffee, one of my daughter's favorite places, is an attractive repurposed home with a wrap around porch and front courtyard. On a nice sunny day, dozens of people were just hanging out on that porch. But most importantly, surrounding this town center were several streets of newly built town homes, in the "New Urbanism" style of organic community. These people spanned generations and cultures, and they all seemed to belong there together. This neighborhood is minutes from DFW airport and adjacent to several large corporate offices, but it felt like you were in the heart of small town America.

An environment that enables year-round physical activity is

also important. This can be a problem in parts of the country that are either too cold in the winter, or too hot in the summer, to enjoy time outdoors. The weather in Buffalo, New York certainly limited what my mother could do in the winter. Physical activity can also be related to the dominant culture of an area. In places like Colorado and the Pacific Northwest, it seems everyone goes hiking or skiing on the weekends. Frederick writes on this topic as well. "An active culture nudges people towards physical activity. We are more likely to be active if those around us are active, and those around us are more active if the environment is conducive to such activity."

Then of course, there is the issue of safety. In determining the fit of a place, it is crucial to examine both internal and external safety factors. Is the home designed for safe living? There are design standards that are specifically geared towards minimizing risk, such as non-slip tiles in bathrooms, grab bars and entrances that do not require stairs. Technological tools, including home monitoring and security systems, personal health monitoring devices and the like can help to ensure that residents are safe. The broader safety of the area, in terms of crime rates, as well as factors such as tornadoes or other severe weather events, relate to the safety of an area.

Access to health care resources is equally important, particularly for an aging society. Is there a good base of primary physicians, urgent care facilities and medical specialists in the area? Are the local hospitals highly rated, and are there teaching institutions for doctors and nurses in the area? Are there specialist health care facilities for heart disease, endocrine disorders, cancer treatment and the like? All of these factors can be critical to ensuring that the place you choose will be a good fit to your health care needs, now and in the future.

Of course, as we discussed earlier in this book, place need not be singular. In today's increasingly mobile world, with remote work and ubiquitous access to technology, it may be possible to live several places. You may have one home base, or even more than one. And you may want to take advantage of an RV or Conversion Van to travel around to the places you want. You might plan extended periods away from your primary place, be it for a few weeks or a few months of the year. We will explore several such options for "multi-locational" living later in this book.

It takes courage to make a change. As Ryan Frederick writes, "one of the challenges of ... planning is that even though we often know what to do, we have a hard time doing it." In the next section of this book we will journey together through planning your own LifeScape. We will explore the dimensions of people, place and purpose, and lay out a financial model that will help you to see how to profit off a change. In the final section, we will put it into practice, helping you design your own Lifescape plan.

Are you ready? Let's get started on your Lifescape solution.

II

The Solution

"I've always been at the right place and the right time.
Of course, I steered myself there."
— Bob Hope

The solution to the problem of place lies in a conscious and deliberate process to identify the variables that are important in your next life move. Armed with this analysis, you can create a Lifescape that builds on place to deliver purpose and surround you with people, all while allowing you to profit, both financially and emotionally, from the experience.

6

What Makes a Good Place

Up to this point, we've spilled a lot of ink on the topic of why a place might be bad — expensive, socially disconnected, and unhealthy. So what makes for a good place?

Any good journalist will tell you to never bury the lede. So here it goes: Buy as small and inexpensive of a home as makes sense, in a walkable, urban community, that you can "lock and leave." Set it up so that you can rent it out when you are not there. This is your home base. Beyond this, design your life to be mobile. Spend a few months of the year away, pursuing enduring relationships, great memories, and delightful weather. In a world that enables many people to work from anywhere, where our families and friends are spread far and wide, and where our interests can draw us to explore this great world, a "semi-nomadic" lifestyle can be the perfect solution to a rich and healthy life.

But make it slow travel; don't just jet off and parachute into some new experience. I am a fan of the flexibility and convenience of RV travel. When it's 105 degrees in Texas, we can pull our trailer up to 7000' in New Mexico or Colorado and relish the cool mountain air. With my Starlink terminal, I get 200Mbps internet while camped in a national forest. But there are other options that can make sense too, like extended "work-cations" where you rent an AirBnB or short-term apartment in another city, perhaps even in another country. My wife's sister has a lake house in Virginia that would be a great place to spend a few weeks. Another old friend has a guest house in the wine country near Paso Robles, California. I work for a company where many of my team are located in Prague, in the Czech Republic. My plan over the next few years is to spend at least a month each year working from that office, where my wife and I also benefit from social relationships with my co-workers and their families, and we can easily take a weekend to visit Krakow, Bratislava, Berlin or Vienna. There are organizations like Remote Year, which provide furnished housing and a co-working membership in great cities of the world for anywhere between a month and a year, traveling with a cohort of 20-30 other remote workers. (I'll go into this in more detail in a later chapter). Every summer my wife and I spend two weeks in Vancouver, auditing courses in theology and religious history at Regent College, coupled with hikes, kayaking, and enjoying the *Bard on the Beach* Shakespeare festival. In 2022 we took courses on Kierkegaard and Wisdom Literature, and in 2023 on the History of Religion in America and the concept of Theosis, all taught by leading experts in these fields. It's kind of geeky, but we enjoy that kind of thing! We have made great friends on these trips. Spending a few months of the year in these locales, with great people, making great memories, is what Lifescapes is all about.

Is Now The Time?

Transitioning to a "right-sized" and "right placed" home is a big decision, and needs due consideration. In his book *Right Place, Right Time*, Ryan Frederick identifies several factors that should be considered in the decision to find a new place to live:

Purpose: Are there things in the location to give meaning to each day? These can include family, work, faith communities, volunteering, etc.

Social Connection: Do you have relationships beyond your immediate family that connect you to the place? Are you able to easily get to these people, ideally without having to drive?

Physical Well-Being: Is the location conducive to outside activities and a healthy lifestyle?

Financial Well-Being: Are you located in a place that is growing and appreciating in value? And are you in the right type and size of home to be able to enjoy it?

These attributes can all be evaluated systematically. Frederick suggests a simple 5-point scorecard for each dimension, from strongly agree to strongly disagree, which can be found on the website of his consulting firm, Here: https://www.here.life/assessment. As you evaluate a potential change, identify the likely score for each of these factors. The scoring algorithm on the here.life website will provide a quick diagnosis of whether it is time for you to move on.

Of course, some of these measures are highly subjective, and it can be important to test the waters before you make a decision that has a high cost if it turns out to be wrong. Frederick advocates for Design Thinking, an approach where you think through an option and then takes steps to validate your assumptions. So, if the idea of downsizing to a town home in a community near family or friends sounds like it fits the bill, first look at renting an AirBnB for several days, including both weekdays and weekends, to get a feel for what it actually is like to live there. But while Frederick's model helps to determine whether it is time to make a move, we take this a step further in Lifescapes, helping you narrow the search to more precisely *where* you should set up your new home base.

A Few Examples

As I mentioned in the previous chapter, one of the key attributes that should be sought in an ideal residential location is accessibility to "Third Places." A Third Place is somewhere other than home and work where you gather with others. This can be a coffee shop, a wine bar, a church, a park, or any location that is convenient, accessible, and conducive to routine social gathering. Ideally, it is somewhere you can walk or bike to. This helps to facilitate what Sheila Liming refers to as "the lost art of hanging out," something we did a lot of as kids and college students, but seem to stop doing when we grow up and buy our nice home in the suburbs.

Let's look at a few examples of residential locales that provide great access to such Third Places and that would score high for many people in the Lifescapes model.

The Cultural District, Ft. Worth, Texas

This area, just west of downtown, is home to several world class museums, the new Dickie's Arena and not far from the Ft. Worth Botanical Gardens and Zoo. But surrounding these cultural amenities are neighborhoods of condos, town homes and single family homes, all with easy access to a wide range of restaurants, coffee shops, a Tom Thumb supermarket, banks and other financial services, a wide range of faith communities, and other retail amenities. The University of North Texas Health Science Center is also located in this area, providing access to high quality medical care. The Trinity River, which divides the Cultural District from downtown, is home to miles of hike and bike trails. Within a 10 minute walk or a 2-3 minute car ride are countless Third Places that make this a model of a healthy urban environment. It is, of course, a city, and there is a somewhat higher incidence of crime than may be experienced in suburban or rural areas, but I have never felt unsafe in the area.

Antiquity, Cornelius, North Carolina

Antiquity is a master planned New Urbanist community adjacent to the historic town center of Cornelius, in the northern suburbs of Charlotte. A few minutes from Lake Norman, one of the most popular boating lakes in the state, Cornelius provides easy access to metropolitan Charlotte, while maintaining a small town feel. Shops, restaurants, churches and a full service supermarket are all a short walk from the homes, town homes, condos and apartments in Antiquity. A network of hike and bike trails also spreads out from the community. Nearby Davidson College provides educational and cultural amenities. And of course this location in Mecklenburg County, North Carolina delivers the benefits of a fast-growing major metropolitan area, with a robust business community centered on banking and financial services, major universities, a hub airport, big league sports, and arts and musical offerings.

Downtown Greenville, South Carolina

Several lists routinely cite Greenville as the best small city in America. *Forbes* magazine named it to their list of the Best Places to Retire in 2023. But it is not just a haven for golfers enjoying their pension. Mid way between Charlotte and Atlanta, this city of 70,000 people in the Upstate region of South Carolina is nestled between Spartanburg and Clemson (home to the eponymous university). Greenville is also home to Furman University, a well regarded liberal arts college. Over the past 25 years, the influx of global companies, including BMW and Michelin's US operations, have transformed this city into an affluent, professional enclave, while retaining a small city feel and an affordable cost of living. Downtown Greenville has seen a large number of new developments, and amenities such as UNITY Park, Flour Field (designed to be reminiscent of Fenway Park and home to the Boston Red Sox affiliated Greenville Drive baseball team) and the 2,100 seat Peace Performing Arts Center. The AMP and Coach Music Factory provide extensive live music venues. Additionally, Greenville has a burgeoning culinary scene, with several famous Charleston restaurateurs expanding to this Upstate city. For outdoor recreation, the Swamp Rabbit Trail provides access from downtown to nearby Falls Park on the Reedy. Sold yet? Chances are a few Greenvillians will be upset that I let the secret out!

Fayetteville, Arkansas

Northwest Arkansas breaks many of the stereotypes associated with The Natural State. Home to the University of Arkansas (Woo Pig Sooie!) and just down the road from the headquarters of Wal-Mart in Bentonville, this delightful town in the Ozark mountain region combines natural beauty with a vibrant local culture and an affordable cost of living. The city has an extensive hike and bike trail system, extending north to Rogers, Springdale and Bentonville. Nearby, Devil's Den State Park and the Boston Mountains offer more opportunities to get out in nature. The Crystal Bridges Museum of Art is home to a world-class collection of American art in a stunning architectural setting, with free general admission. One area where Northwest Arkansas still has room to improve is health care. A 2019 study commissioned by the Northwest Arkansas Council found that the region has good quality and low-cost primary care but has a deficit in high-level specialty care in basically every category, resulting in residents seeking care outside the region. Efforts are underway to create more medical Residency programs to bring young doctors to this area through the University of Arkansas Medical School's Northwest Campus in Fayetteville, to supplement the opportunities available at the state's flagship medical school in Little Rock. But allowing for this one drawback, Fayetteville is a delightful place to live. (Full disclosure, our middle daughter was a Razorback, so we are somewhat biased).

Old Colorado City and Manitou Springs, Colorado

This is a two-fer of areas just west of Colorado Springs. Old Colorado City, a National Historic District, established in 1859, has consistently been voted the Best Neighborhood in Colorado Springs. A thriving arts district on the western edge of the city, Old Colorado City is home to a wide array of galleries, shops, boutiques, inns and restaurants, along with vintage Victorian homes. Manitou Springs is slightly further west, and is more in the mountains. While Colorado Springs is generally considered a car-dependent city, with an average Walk Score of 36, these two communities are exceptions to the rule. Manitou Springs has a Walk Score of 81, meaning that most errands can be accomplished on foot, and Old Colorado City is a Walker's Paradise, with a Walk Score of 92. Big Bear Regional Park and Pike's Peak are nearby, and of course the location on the front range of the Rocky Mountains puts you a short drive from world class skiing or hiking to the top of one of Colorado's many 14ers. The Denver metro area is a short, albeit often stressful, drive up I-25, providing further access to sports, cultural, educational and professional resources, and a major hub airport.

The Lifescapes Model

Ultimately, determining whether a given place is right for you requires some homework. Thankfully, we have made this process somewhat easier, with the Lifescapes Model, a quantitative scoring system that helps you to evaluate a set of choices and make the right decision. Using a technique called SMARTER (Simple Multi-Attribute Rating Technique Employing Rankings), the Lifescapes Model allows you to compare multiple potential places, evaluated on a set of key attributes, and generate an Aggregate Benefit Score. to use the model, visit our website at www.Lifescapes.info, where you can input the criteria that are important to you and find the neighborhoods that best suit your needs.

Using the Lifescapes model, you can narrow the consideration set and identify a set of places that will enable you to thrive. You might be surprised by what the model serves up for you.

There are several variables that go into the Lifescapes model, making use of the best, up-to-date resources to evaluate the attractiveness of a given locale. These include:

- **Active Lifestyle**

Using data from Redfin's WalkScore and BikeScore database, look for a location that is easy to get around without a car.

- **Health and Educational Resources**

As you age, access to top quality medical practitioners becomes increasingly important. Communities are scored in the Lifescapes model based on rates of doctors, dentists and mental health providers per 100,000 people, and receive additional points for having a medical school or large teaching hospital within the County. Other factors related to health included in the Lifescapes model are air and water quality and access to outdoor recreation. Additionally, the presence of one or more large universities or liberal arts colleges and an above-average share of college educated people in the area factor into the model.

- **Safety**

CrimeGrades.org provides ZIP code level data on both violent crime and property crimes. While crime can be highly localized and vary considerably within a ZIP code, it is helpful to focus on areas with an A or B CrimeGrade score. Importantly, a C is average on Crime Grades, so neighborhoods with a C or C- should not necessarily be discounted.

- **Weather and Natural Disasters**

Some great towns, like Madison, Wisconsin, are delightful in the summer but can be pretty rough in the winter. At the same time, many people find the heat and humidity of Florida and Texas unbearable come the summer months. And of course, hurricanes, blizzards, tornadoes and earthquakes can devastate a community. Data on average monthly temperature, coupled with rates of disasters and severe weather events, help to identify Goldilocks locales. A proxy for destructive weather risk is the average homeowner's insurance rate, which tends to be much higher in areas that are prone to tornadoes, hail storms or other weather-related risks.

- **Cost of Living and Economic Prospects**

Is the area growing or shrinking? How fast are home values increasing? Is housing affordable? These variables are key to ensuring a successful long-term financial return on real estate. The goal is to identify areas with high growth potential where homes in great communities are still priced at or below the national average.

- **Cultural Amenities**

How important to you are the presence of major league sports teams, a performing arts center with a resident symphony or opera company, James Beard-award winning restaurants, or other cultural amenities? Each of these variables can factor in to your choice of an ideal location.

The weights applied to these factors can vary from person to person, and are often conditioned by family or other personal considerations that will pull you to a region of the country or a particular type of locale. Sometimes the results are surprising.

Within the Lifescapes Model, you can set the rank order of the attributes, or choose to ignore some while including others. Once you narrow down your consideration set, the Lifescapes Model generates scores that show you which area scores highest on the factors that are most important to you.

7

Lock, Leave, Love

One of the key features of the Lifescapes model is the ability to be a nomad, or at least semi-nomadic, migrating between a home base and other locales that fit your needs for fellowship, fun or financial opportunity. In today's world, it is increasingly straightforward to have one primary residence coupled with spending meaningful time wherever it is 70 degrees and sunny.

The Encyclopedia Britannica defines nomadism as:

> *A way of life of peoples who do not live continually in the same place but move cyclically or periodically. ... Nomadism does not imply unrestricted and undirected wandering; rather, it is based on temporary centers whose stability depends on the availability of food supply and the technology for exploiting it.*

This lifestyle, the Encyclopedia Britannica notes, declined steadily in the 20th century for economic and political reasons, including the spread of systematic agriculture, the growth of industry, and the policies of governments that view nomadism as incompatible with modern life. But as the 21st century has progressed, we have seen the emergence of a new type of nomadic lifestyle, one that is no longer dependent on the availability of food, but rather on access to a high-speed internet connection.

Most people are well-acquainted with the concept of the digital nomad. These are people who combine working remotely with travel, often spending years on the move, journeying across countries and even continents. A 2022 research study by MBO Partners found that 16.9 million American workers currently describe themselves as digital nomads, increasing 9% from 2021 and a staggering 131% from the pre-pandemic year 2019.[12]

The stereotypical image of the digital nomad is a young, male, self-employed in an eCommerce or digital creative business. The idea was popularized by Tim Ferris' wildly successful book, *The 4-Hour Workweek*, originally published in 2007. Ferris shared his own experience of creating a lifestyle business that allowed him to travel the world, pursue his passions, and outsource his tasks to low-cost virtual assistants. Sounds great, but don't get your hopes up. A 2012 *Harvard Business Review* article concluded that the premise behind Ferris' book is a "fantasy."[13] There is no substitute for putting meaningful time behind your work, and even Ferris has publicly stated that many of the ideas in his book are not broadly feasible. Others have pointed to profound ethical issues with Ferris' use of low-paid overseas virtual assistants, along with the burn-out experienced by these virtual assistants trying to keep up with Ferris' incessant, non-stop work demands.[14] So while the idea of making tens of thousands of dollar a month by selling stuff through Facebook ads that gets drop-shipped from China probably isn't a viable strategy for most people, Ferris' core notion that work need not be location dependent is even more relevant today than when he first argued for it in 2007. Many far more realistic opportunities for nomadic work have emerged in the post-pandemic era, ranging from travel nurses (who work short gigs at medical facilities in different locales), to any of a range of professions that can be done effectively from anywhere. In my own profession, running a market research technology firm with teams in Europe, North America, and Asia, no one really cares where I am physically sitting on any given day. In my wife's field of accounting, skills such as being an Intuit-Certified Quickbooks consultant or a fractional CFO can easily fit into a nomadic lifestyle. Others teach remotely from the road, do sales support, handle medical billing, write code, manage digital media — the list goes on.

As the MBO Research report concludes, "people who embrace a location-independent, technology-enabled lifestyle – have moved from being eccentrics to mainstream in less than a decade." Today, nomadic workers range across many industries and defy demographic stereotypes. The number of digital nomads with a traditional wage and salary job doubled in 2020, and increased by another 42% in 2021. One-in-ten digital nomads currently are over the age of 60, and this group is growing steadily. The COVID-19 pandemic unleashed many professionals from the requirement to report to a physical office, and also fed a profound realization that the risk of premature death requires a rethinking of the priorities of life — one of which is the ability to balance the need to work with the desire to live where you want and to have meaningful time with family and friends. Whether its full-time remote work, or a periodic "workation" in an enjoyable location, the goal is to be semi-nomadic in your lifestyle.

The Need for a Home Base

While a purely nomadic life may seem attractive, the reality is that a home base is typically a requirement. It is possible to get a virtual mailbox and not have a single permanent address. (We cover several options for such services in the Appendix). There is a small subset of families who live full-time on the road. You can follow several of their adventures on YouTube, including our favorites — Keep Your Daydream, Happily Ever Hanks and Switch it Up. But there are several key advantages to a semi-nomadic lifestyle with a clearly defined primary residence:

- Many of your most important family and community relationships may be rooted in a particular geographic area.
- It can be essential to maintain relationships with a primary physician, dentist and other medical professionals in a specific location.
- Financial services, such as banking and insurance, may be tied to a specific area. Health insurance, for instance, is regulated at the State level, so the choice of your domicile State may determine the kinds of plans that are available to you. Some banks, moreover, may refuse to do business with people who do not have a fixed, permanent address.
- A primary residence is a store of wealth and appreciates in value. A key element to the Lifescapes model is to not have too much equity in a home, but trading down to a "lock and leave" place can enable long-term, tax favored asset appreciation.
- Taxes vary considerably from State to State, and the choice

> between a few options for a legal domicile may result in a variance of several thousand dollars per year. We will go into more detail on total effective tax burden by State in the next chapter.

This need for a home base played out in a very real way for Jeff and Patti Kinzbach, hosts of the "Rocking the RV Life" podcast. Jeff, a retired rock music DJ from Cleveland, noticed in early 2023 that he was increasingly fatigued and experiencing shortness of breath while walking outdoors. He had always been in excellent health and wasn't sure at first what to make of the symptoms, until he started feeling numbness in his arm on a hike. He returned to his Cleveland home base, where his primary physician ordered several tests and referred him to a cardiologist, who determined he needed open heart surgery for a triple bypass. This is the kind of reality that is generally not talked about by those who promote the globetrotting digital nomad life. Jeff was very thankful for the excellent medical facilities available to him near his home base in Cleveland.

Beyond these significant, practical considerations, it is simply a reality that people thrive best when rooted in a community. This does not mean that you can't escape the heat and humidity of the south eastern United States for the cool mountain air of the Rockies, British Columbia or the Finger Lakes of New York for a few months each summer, or flee the snow of Madison, Wisconsin or Burlington, Vermont between December and April. But you want to design in flexibility — the ability to close up and leave your home base and go off in pursuit of 70 and Sunny.

For our personal Lifescape, my wife and I see a need to maintain our primary residence in the Dallas area for a few more years, while spending two weeks every summer in Vancouver and taking extended workcations to southern Colorado, the Beaver's Bend area of southeastern Oklahoma, and Prague. When it's 105 in Dallas, we will be in British Columbia or up in the Rockies. We will camp in the Ouachita Mountains in the Fall, connecting to work over Starlink. We'll shop the Christmas Market on Wenceslas Square. We may decide to relocate our home base in a few years, once our youngest has graduated college and our 2nd daughter finishes law school. Their decision where they choose to establish their next home may influence our choice of a new home base.

Lock it and Leave it

"Lock and Leave" is one of the hottest trends in real estate. As an article on Neighborhoods.com states, "This style of homeownership is built for convenience and security, allowing people to own a home while enjoying the freedom of very few maintenance responsibilities. Homebuyers want residences that reflect their lifestyles, and for both active baby boomers and adventurous millennials, this means smaller homes with amenities or automation systems that enable an on-the-go lifestyle."[15] For decades, the average size of American homes has been increasing. But for people who want more flexibility in their life, less is more.

I first heard the term about 15 years ago, when my friends Bill and Connie were looking to sell their large, single family home in Franklin, Tennessee. Bill worked for an international organization that had him managing a project in Cape Town, South Africa for several months at a time. Connie also had an increasing need to spend time with her aging parents in Gallup,

New Mexico. Their kids were grown and heading off to college, and Bill explained to me that he needed a place he could lock and leave, without the need to care for a lawn or any other exterior maintenance. Unsure of the ultimate plan, they leased out their primary home for a few years, with the lease payments more than covering the cost of an apartment they maintained for when they were back in Nashville. At that time, this was the best option for a lock and leave. But as we'll see, there are many other options today.

The typical concept of a lock and leave home is a condominium or town home. But newer developments offer options for semi-detached villas and even smaller single family homes in communities where all exterior maintenance is handled by the HOA, and even services like mail scanning and pet sitting can be arranged through the community.

Technology has made lock and leave housing even more practical. Home automation hubs such as Samsung SmartThings, Google Nest Hub, Savant, and any number of applications that can be accessed through Amazon's Alexa, enable security systems, thermostats and lights to be managed from anywhere in the world. These systems provide real time alerts if something like a power outage, fire or a water leak occurs. If friends or family — or an AirBnB guest — will be at your house while you are away, smart home technology can set new codes to unlock the doors, adjust the temperature, raise the blinds and ensure the lights are turned out when they leave. Some builders are now creating entire new home communities with these features built in, such as Lennar Homes' Wi-Fi Certified Smart Homes. In South Austin, Lennar created a 400-home community of condos, townhomes, lofts and single family homes, The Enclave at Estancia, with Amazon Alexa voice-recognition technology built into each home. This is just one example of the innovations that are reshaping the housing market to enable a more nomadic lifestyle.

Cashflowing Your Home

One of the greatest innovations in residential real estate in the past 15 years has been the ability to generate passive income from a home through short term rentals. In 2007, roommates Joe Gebbia and Brian Chesky were having trouble affording the rent on their San Francisco apartment, so they came up with the idea of allowing out of town convention visitors to pay for the right to sleep on an air mattress in their living room. The business they built from this basic idea, AirBnB, now has a market cap of over $90 billion.

Allowing your primary residence to be rented out on AirBnB (or VRBO or any of several other short term rental platforms) is not for everyone. But as a component of a Lifescapes plan, a properly situated, lock and leave residence, equipped with a home automation system, can allow your primary residence to pay for itself.

One great example of cashflowing residences is Marc and Trisha Leach of the popular RV YouTube channel "Keep Your Daydream." The Leaches have traveled nearly full time in their RV for several years after selling their home in Phoenix. However, they felt the need for a home base where they could gather as a family at the holidays or just to regroup. They now have two home bases: a cabin in the mountains outside Flagstaff, Arizona, and a beach bungalow in Florida. They have made Florida their legal domicile for tax purposes. Both homes are set up to be rented out when they are in their RV, using the

Lodgify platform (lodgify.com). Marc told me in an email that a third home, potentially in Michigan, might be in their future plans. For Thanksgiving through New Years of 2022, the Leaches were at their cabin in Flagstaff. Later in the Spring of 2023 they were overseeing renovations to the bungalow in Florida. But when they are traveling in their RV, these properties are making money for them.

The key factors in the viability of a home as a short term rental, or course, are the location, size, up front costs of setting it up for guests, and the target audience of renters. As Jacob Harvey writes in *Airbnb Business*, "the most successful Airbnb properties are often located in popular cities for tourism or remote areas of the country that attract hikers and peace seekers." It will be essential to furnish the property with appropriate items for short term guests, market it properly and of course secure any personal valuables (in a deadbolted closet or off site storage space) during the times that you are not there. Reliable cleaning and maintenance services will need to be contracted. The property will not manage itself, but with good technology, a solid support structure, and proper setup, the home can quickly turn cashflow positive. A basic, free calculator available on AirDna.co will allow you to see how much nightly rental income, and what likely occupancy rate, can be expected from any address in the United States. Of course, there are state and local laws regulating short term rentals that are constantly in flux, and market demand can also be unpredictable. And if a home is used as a rental property, the rental income will be subject to self employment tax and any eventual gain on the sale of the property will be subject to capital gains tax. There is a lot to think about if you intend to utilize your primary residence as a short term rental property, but the cashflow it opens up can create some great possibilities.

So, now that we have addressed the What of Lifescapes, we will turn next to the question of Where.

8

There's No Place Like Home

Up to this point, we have covered the Why and the What of Lifescapes — fleeing the subdivision, freeing up capital, and fixing your sights on a semi-nomadic lifestyle. But now we must turn our attention to the critical question of Where. Faced with innumerable options for a place to live, how do we narrow down the choices and identify a home base that checks all the right boxes?

Back in Chapter 6, "What Makes a Good Place," I covered some of the key questions that should go into selecting your home base location. A few of these questions include:

- Does it support a physically active lifestyle?
- Are there excellent health care resources in the community?
- Is it safe?
- Is it affordable, yet in a growing market?
- Does it offer cultural, sports and educational options that align to your interests?
- How are the schools in the area?
- How is the climate? Is there significant risk of environmen-

tal disasters (earthquakes, hurricanes, floods, tornadoes) or adverse impacts of climate change?

Some of these questions might be non-negotiables for you: for instance, you may feel that you need live in an area with professional sports teams, or in a town that is home to a large university, or that has a resident symphony. You may want to avoid areas prone to hurricanes or tornadoes. While you might be an empty-nester, the reputation of local schools can be an important consideration in the overall quality of the neighborhood and the resale potential of the property. And of course you may have to limit your consideration set to a particular metropolitan area, a State or a region of the country that is in proximity to close family or friends.

Trigger warning for those of you still recovering from math class: this is going to get a bit technical. I'm going to lay out a quantitative methodology for computing a score for a set of places, and then determining which place best fits your priorities. If your eyes glaze over reading the next few paragraphs, don't worry, it will be over soon. I'll show you my own real-life example, where the math will hopefully make a lot more sense. And if you use the user interface on Lifescapes.Info, you will just point and click and all the math is done for you.

Lifescapes offers a systematic approach to evaluating the variables behind the question of where you should live. The model is based on a decision analysis technique called SMARTER — Simple Multi-Attribute Rating Technique Exploiting Ranks.[16] The technique works as follows:

1. Select the attributes that factor into your decision
2. Rank order these attributes in their order of importance to

you

3. For a set of choices, identify the quantitative scores for each attribute. For some things, this can be a zero or one (something is present or not). For others, it is a scaled number, such as the population growth rate, the neighborhood WalkScore, or the GreatSchools rating of the local high school. Sometimes, the scoring needs to be entirely subjective, with your own low/medium/high score assigned to each option.
4. Each of these scores then needs to be indexed to 100. The best option is scored at 100, the worst is scored 0, and the scores for all other options are recalibrated to their percent difference between these extremes. Variables like WalkScore are already indexed, but others require a little bit of math. If the average homeowners insurance annual premium (a good proxy for weather and disaster risk) between three potential locations, for instance, is $2,000, $2,500, and $3,000, then the option at $2,000 would get a score of 100, the option at $3,000 would be scored 0, and the option at $2,500 would be scored 50. Importantly, this math is already done for you, using the best available data sources, in the Lifescapes model. But of course, if you have variables that are important to you that are not built into Lifescapes, you can always work the math yourself.
5. Each 0-100 score is then multiplied by a Rank Order Centroid (ROC Weight), which varies based on the number of attributes being considered. If only two attributes are important to you, the score for the first is multiplied by 75% and the score for the second by 25%. If there are three important attributes, the first score is multiplied by 61.1%, the second by 27.8%, and the third by 11.1%. You'll

notice that these ROC Weights always add up to 100%. The Lifescapes model allows up to 7 attributes to be factored into your rank order of importance. If you make use of the automated scoring model on Lifescapes.info, the math is all done for you once you select your potential locations and the rank order of your important attributes.

6. The indexed score for each attribute is multiplied by each ROC weight, and the results are summed to generate an Aggregate Benefit Score — ABS — which can be used to compare the set of options and determine which is best. The attribute you rank most important always gets the biggest ROC Weight, meaning that it factors the most into the resulting ABS score.

The Rank Order Centroids — ROC Weights — are an important part of the calculation. They weight the indexed score for each attribute in your decision by its relative, rank-ordered importance. The ROC Weights are shown below for decisions based on between two and seven attributes.

ROC Weights

	Number of Attributes					
Rank	2	3	4	5	6	7
1	75.0%	61.1%	52.1%	45.7%	40.8%	37.0%
2	25.0%	27.8%	27.1%	25.7%	24.2%	22.8%
3		11.1%	14.6%	15.7%	15.8%	15.6%
4			6.3%	9.0%	10.3%	10.9%
5				4.0%	6.1%	7.3%
6					2.8%	4.4%
7						2.0%

As an example, let's say you are making a decision between two locations based on three attributes: walkability, the quality of the schools and the presence of a major performing arts center in the county. If the WalkScores were 20 for the first option and 80 for the second, the GreatSchools score was 6 out of 10 for Option A and 8 out of 10 for Option B (60 and 80 when transformed to a 0–100 scale), and one location had a symphony center and the other did not, the calculation would be as follows:

Option A:

Walkability 20 * .611 = 20.6
Schools 60 * .278 = 16.7
Perf Arts 100 * .111 = 11.1
Aggregate Benefit Score = **48.4**

Option B:

Walkability 80 * .611 = 48.9
Schools 80 * .278 = 22.2
Perf Arts 0 * .111 = 0
Aggregate Benefit Score = **51.1**

So, Option B is the winner. The better walkability and schools outweigh the impact of the performing arts center.

Now, suppose you reverse the rank order of importance of the attributes, where the performing arts center is now the most important, schools is second most important, and walkability third. Reworking the calculation, it works out as follows:

Option A:

Perf Arts 100 * .611 = 61.1
Schools 60 * .278 = 16.7
Walkability 20 * .111 = 2.2

Aggregate Benefit Score = **80.0**

Option B:

Perf Arts 0 * .611 = 0
Schools 80 * .278 = 22.2
Walkability 80 * .111 = 8.9
Aggregate Benefit Score = **31.1**

With this change to the rank order importance, Option A is chosen. It should be clear that the choice of attributes and your subjective judgment as to their relative importance is critical to the outcome of the exercise. But the great thing is that Lifescapes enables you to change the set of attributes that are important to you and to adjust their relative rankings, to explore how this impacts your decision. As a planning and evaluation tool, this is an unprecedented step forward in the process of identifying the place that is right for you.

It is important to note that price of a home in each location is not factored into the model. Instead, the ABS Score is calculated based on the relative performance of the rank-ordered attributes of the location, regardless of price. Then, the scores are compared to price on a simple graph, with ABS on the X axis and price on the Y axis. This reveals areas of relative value — options where paying a lower price trades off with little or no change in the Aggregate Benefit Score. The line from the lowest to the highest scoring ABS is known as the Efficient Frontier. Any option lying below the Efficient Frontier represents an excellent value for money, while options above the Efficient Frontier are relatively expensive for the value they deliver. In the example above, with the first set of rank ordered attributes, the resulting scores were relatively close to one another. Looking at these in relation to the cost of housing in each area might lead you to conclude that you would trade off a slightly lower Aggregate Benefit Score for a lower cost of a target home, getting relatively more bang for your buck.

OK, that's a lot of technical discussion. Let's bring it to life in my own, real world example.

We have a requirement to remain in the Dallas-Ft. Worth metropolitan area, and we narrowed down our consideration set to five potential areas of the Metroplex, all of which met the base criteria of being walkable and accessible to a wide range of "third places," along with lots of high density, lock-and-leave housing.

1. The Cultural District of Fort Worth (76107)
2. The Riverwalk in Flower Mound (75028)
3. Old Town Lewisville (75057)
4. Old Town Coppell (75019)
5. Frisco Square (75033)

Our our case, we selected five decision attributes. In rank order, these are:

1. Walkability (the WalkScore rating)
2. Safety (Crime Grades data, A-F scores transformed to a 0-100 index)
3. Quality of Schools (GreatSchools rating of the local high school)
4. Presence of a performing arts center in the county (100 if home to a resident professional symphony or opera company, 50 if a local performing arts center with at least 300 seats, 0 if none)

5. Quality of health care in the County (my custom score, based on data from the University of Wisconsin's County Health Rankings plus bonus points for having a medical school in the County, which is a proxy for access to specialized medical care)

Other people, of course, could have a different set of attributes that are important in their decision. For instance, you might not be drawn to a performing arts center, but place a high value of the presence of professional sports teams. You may be willing to forgo good local schools in exchange for great healthcare resources in the County. These attributes, and more, are available in Lifescapes and can be applied to your own evaluation.

So, here are the results for us:

		Ft. Worth	Flower Mound	Lewisville	Coppell	Frisco
Attribute	ROC Weight	76107	75028	75057	75019	75033
Walkability	0.46	88	62	61	47	70
Safety	0.26	25	100	70	90	80
Schools	0.16	30	70	30	70	70
Performing Arts	0.09	100	0	50	50	0
Health Factors	0.04	85	65	65	65	85
Aggregate Benefit Score		**64**	**68**	**58**	**63**	**67**
Target Home Price		*$600,000*	*$550,000*	*$375,000*	*$700,000*	*$500,000*

Data current as of August, 2023

The graph below shows the relationship between target home price and Aggregate Benefit Score, with the line between Lewisville (lowest ABS) and Flower Mound (highest) representing the Efficient Frontier. Coppell and Ft. Worth are above the Efficient Frontier, indicating that the price of homes in these areas are expensive relative to the benefits they deliver (using my selected, rank-ordered criteria). Townhomes on the market in Frisco Square are priced relatively efficiently in relation to the benefits offered by that community.

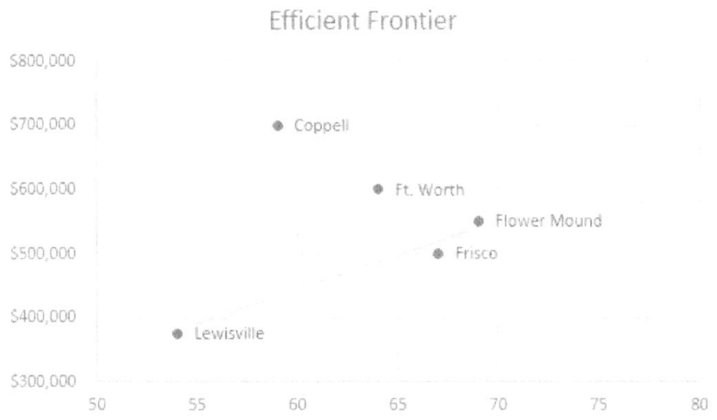

The results of this calculation were somewhat surprising to us. We were really drawn to the Cultural District of Ft. Worth, with the amazing, world-class museums and great "hang out" options all within an easy walking distance of several nice, new townhome developments. It has by far the highest WalkScore. Nearby, Bass Performance Hall is home to the annual Opera Festival, as well as the world-renowned Cliburn International Piano Competition. We had looked at several options ranging between $450,000 and $850,000 and spent a few afternoons getting a feel for the neighborhood. We hiked the Trinity River trail. But all these great, positive features traded off with some of the downsides of being in a large city, in terms of crime risk and lower rated schools. The net result was that based on our criteria, Ft. Worth came in third overall. And in terms of home prices versus the aggregate benefit score from living in the area, the Ft. Worth Cultural District was high priced.

We had also been intrigued by the Old Town areas of Coppell and Lewisville. Old Town Coppell has a great coffee shop, several restaurants and a brand new, 400-seat community performing arts center. The local schools are first rate. It is minutes from DFW Airport. But walkability is limited, with no supermarkets within walking distance. And it is by far the most expensive option. Old Town Lewisville is home to the Lewisville Grand Theater and has been the scene of substantial redevelopment of late. It has a station on the DCTA A-Train, connecting Denton with the Dallas Area Rapid Transit system. There are several brand new townhomes at a very attractive price point. But the local high school scores a 3 on the GreatSchools rating, and the walkability was not as great as some other areas (again, no supermarket you can walk to), pulling the ABS down.

The surprising winner was the Flower Mound Riverwalk. This location is still being built out in 2023, so it takes a little foresight to see what it will become. But this neighborhood of townhomes adjacent to a creek lined with restaurants and linked to an extensive trail network, is also a short walk to a Market Street supermarket. A hospital and two hotels adjoin the development. Marcus High School is first rate. It also turns out to be the closest of the options to where we already live, and is very close to the church we attend. But I promise, we didn't cook the books to reach this conclusion. We were prepared to move much further away. But the data points to the Riverwalk. And at the available price point, we could sell our appreciated home, pay cash in this community, and have money to spare.

Frisco Square is a close second, with excellent walkability, a relatively safe environment, great schools and excellent health care resources. For anyone who prioritizes sports, the FC Dallas major league soccer team plays across the street at Toyota Stadium and Dr. Pepper Park, home to the Frisco Roughriders minor league baseball team, is a short drive down the Dallas North Tollway. But the city lacks any meaningful venue for performing arts, which is a real negative for us. At the same time, the Ft. Worth Cultural District remains an intriguing 3rd place option, despite the higher cost. We could be persuaded to go with this option as well. Most importantly, the SMARTER analysis has enabled us to quantify our subjective judgments and look at the trade offs in a systematic manner, narrowing the question of "where" to a data-driven decision.

Of course, as anyone who has lived in Texas can attest, the summers are miserable, with temperatures over 100 for weeks on end. And the winters can be yucky as well. So while the Riverwalk represents an ideal home base, we can lock the place up and leave it for several weeks in the summer to head to Colorado or Canada, and in the winter you may find us anywhere from Prague to Peru.

9

Community

"Some people think they are in community, but they are only in proximity. True community requires commitment and openness. It is a willingness to extend yourself to encounter and know the other." –David Spangler

Community is one of the most important elements of a healthy and productive life. The Lifescapes tagline is "Find Your Place, Live Your Dream." While the previous chapter focused on how to identify a walkable community that aligns with your priorities, we will now turn our attention to how to make it work for you — how to break through the isolation that pervades suburban life and build meaningful and impactful relationships in both our home base and across a semi-nomadic lifestyle. In the quote above from New Age mystic David Spangler, he points to two key success factors: commitment and openness. It takes some work to engage with and build community, and it requires the participant to take some risks and expose some vulnerability.

Loneliness and isolation are a public health crisis. The U.S. Surgeon General, Dr. Vivek Murthy, has raised an alarm about the devastating effect of the "epidemic of loneliness." Dr. Murthy describes loneliness as "an underappreciated public health crisis that has harmed individual and societal health. Our relationships are a source of healing and well-being hiding in plain sight – one that can help us live healthier, more fulfilled, and more productive lives."[17] Beyond the clear impact of loneliness on mental health, The Surgeon General's report states that poor or insufficient social connections are associated with a 29% increased risk of heart disease, a 32% increased risk of stroke, and a 50% increased risk of developing dementia for older adults. Additionally, lacking social connection increases risk of premature death by more than 60%.

Up to this point, I have emphasized the physical and financial benefits that can be obtained from finding the right kind of place to establish as your home base, while also enabling a semi-nomadic lifestyle. But there are several aspects that need to be kept in mind that relate to how to engineer a life in community.

I have been influenced by two parties. First, an old friend of mine sent me an email where he questioned the idea of being overly nomadic. He suggested that I was missing the point of maintaining strong family and community connections. Secondly, my respected colleague Ryan Frederick, the author of *Right Place, Right Time*, wrote a blog post in August 2023 with the headline "You Were Not Meant to Thrive Everywhere." To quote:

> *A decision about home is not just about your physical dwelling (i.e., your four walls), it also is a decision about neighborhood which can have a profound impact. A*

> *key question is whether a neighborhood is made up of people like you. There is robust research that shows how commonalities facilitate friendship. People are simply more likely to befriend others of the same gender, age, ethnicity, and so on. Taken too far, however, a community of people composed of people just like you could be stifling and boring. Perhaps a better question is whether a neighborhood is made up of* enough *people like you that you can spark friendships with.*

These twin inputs caused me to take a critical look at the idea of nomadism. While I value geographic flexibility — the ability to lock-and-leave a primary residence and spend a few weeks or months on the road — the reason for this was not mobility *per se*, some sort of Jack Kerouac *On The Road* mystique, but rather the ability to foster and re-engage with the important relationships in our lives. Kerouac famously wrote "Nothing behind me, everything ahead of me, as is ever so on the road." But I contend that we have a lot behind us and that in a geographically dispersed society such as we have in the western world, a key element of a healthy lifestyle can be the ability to spend *quantity time* with people we have known along the way.

My children all live in different States, as do all of our extended family and many of our dearest friends. I don't just want to be a digital nomad. But I want the flexibility to lock up my home and pull our travel trailer out to see our daughter in Utah, or my wife's sisters in Virginia. For the past 5 years I have worked for a company based in the Czech Republic, and I have many great professional and personal relationships there. So maybe I want to spend a month every year in Prague.

But we all need a place that is home. We have chosen to remain in the Dallas metroplex for at least the next few years — in part because our graduate-school-aged children are still very much in flux as to where they will settle down. We have friendships here, a church community, professional relationships such as our physicians, dentist, and the like, and a wealth of amenities such as the Dallas Symphony and the Ft. Worth Opera Festival that we enjoy. And being in the fastest growing metro area of the fastest growing state in America offers the promise of meaningful home value appreciation in the coming years. Using the Lifescapes Model, we found a neighborhood close by that had not even been on our radar until I started on this book. It is walking distance to our favorite supermarket, great restaurants, a coffee place and wine bar, a nail salon, medical providers, a dog groomer and more, and also has access to an extensive hike and bike trail system that extends over 10 miles north and south. It is zoned for a highly-rated high school. Even though we are empty-nesters, we recognize that this factor will help with any eventual sale. And it's actually closer to our church, my wife's job, and several of our friends than we were before. Moving to this neighborhood checked all the boxes for our requirements for place.

The question then becomes *how* we build community in a place. Tracy Bowers, PhD, a senior contributor to *Forbes*, addressed this topic in an October 2020 article.[18] She focuses on three key factors: purpose, belonging and resilience. Purpose means keeping in mind your objectives for involvement in the community and the value of your contribution. This doesn't have to mean that you are the lead volunteer for every community need. But it can mean that you view yourself as a valuable part of your community and find ways to make a meaningful contribution. This can mean being a good neighbor, helping out where you can and being involved in decisions that impact your neighborhood. Belonging refers to the process of becoming tight-knit into a community. You need to be willing to invest time and energy into the relationships that define your community — be it in person or virtual. Simple gestures, like thank you notes, can be critical components of creating a sense of belonging. In a world of text messaging, making the effort to meet up in-person, or (God forbid!) using your smartphone to actually place a call, deepens the bonds between people.[19] Resilience refers to being willing to take risks, accept the occasional failure, and learn from adversity that occurs with both you and those around you. It also means having an openness to those with different experience and perspective, often drawn from a different cultural background. Sometimes, putting ourselves in too much of a bubble can hinder our growth, as we insulate ourselves from risk or challenges to our thinking.

Living in a walkable community can help with all of these objectives — purpose, belonging and resilience — by breaking down some of the physical barriers that lead to isolation. A study published in the journal *Health & Place*, which analyzed data from a survey of 1,745 adults in 32 neighborhoods across Seattle, Baltimore and Washington, DC found a strong correlation between walkability and social cohesion. Similarly, a study published in the *American Journal of Public Health* found that people living in walkable neighborhoods were more likely to know their neighbors, participate politically, trust others, and be socially engaged. As we walk around and get to know our neighbors, we build the kind of "social capital" that creates trust and mutual care between people.[20]

Of course, this doesn't just happen. There are some concrete steps you can take to create purpose and belonging in a neighborhood.

- Make the effort to introduce yourself to your neighbors and learn about their lives. There is a phrase that I was taught once in a sales training seminar that has served me well in many areas of life: "Be interested, not interesting."
- Join a local sports team or some other type of club. I'm always amazed by my college friend and avid Real Madrid fan Francisco, who continues to play soccer with his local "geezer team" even as he fast approaches 60 years of age.
- Go to church (or synagogue, temple or mosque...). Even if this has not been a big part of your life, or if your belief system is not all that certain, this can be a place of deep community and mutual care. After all, community and communion share the same root word. These are places where people confront the most important questions of life, and where the fundamental purpose is to draw closer to one another as you draw close to God.
- Find out where you can serve. It might be an animal shelter, a youth sports league, or a senior center — but there is undoubtedly an organization in your community where your skills and experience, or just your willing pair of hands, can make a difference.
- Be purposeful in your social outreach. That friend you haven't talked to in a year — pick up the phone. That neighbor down the street, invite them over. My wife and I have made it a priority to make at least one social outreach to someone we haven't seen in a while each week. We refuse to let the busyness of daily life get in the way of social connection.

But of course part of the basic premise of this book is that a semi-nomadic lifestyle can also build community. It is not uncommon for many families to live in geographically disparate locales. Over the past several years, I had children in Chicago, Fayetteville, Arkansas and Salt Lake City, and family in Buffalo, Orange County, California, northern Virginia and the west coast of Florida. Working remotely (at least part of the time) and being able to lock up a place and leave for weeks at a time allows for more than just a flying visit. And we really like being able to travel by RV, so that we come with our own bed and bathroom. We are able to spend meaningful time with our family and friends without imposing at all.

It is also possible to build strong and meaningful communities with others enjoying a nomadic lifestyle. One of the oldest and largest groups of recreational vehicle enthusiasts is the Escapees Club (members refer to themselves as S-K-Ps). This organization provides some specific services to members, such as setting up legal domiciles and mail forwarding services for people who are on the road for extended periods. They also have a sub-group catering to GenX, working age adults, called Xscapers. Escapees hosts events throughout the year, some tied to big outdoor enthusiast happenings such as the Albuquerque Balloon Fiesta. But it also sponsors a vast array of affinity groups, called Birds of a Feather ("BOF"). These run the gamut, with just the start of the alphabet covering alternative medicine, amateur radio, aviation history, bikes and Boomers. Any SKP can join a BOF group aligned to their interests. And if one does not exist for your specific affinity, you can create one.

There are several other of these mobile lifestyle affinity communities. Fans of the full-time RV living YouTube channel "Switch it Up" can join the SwitchCrew, which hosts meet-ups several times a year. There is also E3 Camping, which focuses on education and empowerment for people interested in RV living, with an active discussion forum and regional gatherings. One app that I am starting to use is called Nomad Near Me, available in the Apple and Google Play app stores. This allows me to connect with friends who are also traveling around, or to establish connections with interesting people I meet along the way, and alerts me if we happen to be in the same area again.

Beyond the RV community, there are several ways in which a semi-nomadic lifestyle can be organized to help build relationships. Organizations like Road Scholar host educational travel, geared primarily to retirees but also an option for working-age adults. Another to consider, if you are able to work remotely for at least a month at time, is Remote Year.

I first encountered Remote Year back in 2016. I was in the New Orleans airport, sitting at the bar as my flight to Chicago was delayed by heavy thunderstorms. I struck up a conversation with two people sitting next to me. One was a very nice, young, Australian woman. I asked what brought her to New Orleans and why she was headed to Chicago. She told me that she had just finished Remote Year - where she traveled with a group of around 30 people, spending a month at a time in a different city of the world. The organization provided furnished apartments and a co-working facility, and arranged group activities every weekend. She was able to work full time for her company in Australia, logging in from Cape Town, Buenos Aires, Kyoto and Seville. Over the course of the year, she created very deep and meaningful relationships with people who came and went from the cohort, and now she was visiting a few of them in America.

This program was intriguing, and I've continued to look into Remote Year as they have grown and diversified their programs.

You can join for a month, 4 months, or an entire year, as you see fit. Participants range from their young 20s to over 70, with mostly singles but some married couples as well. The program is particularly appealing to female digital nomads, who are able to travel and explore new cultures, while also feeling a greater sense of physical safety and security than they might experience traveling alone. A friend of mine who does not have very close family connections, which tends to make the holidays awkward, took my advice and joined a Remote Year program in Medellin, Columbia in December 2022. He joined about 25 others from around the world and built some great, lasting relationships.

These are just a few ideas of the myriad ways that we can both design our place and leverage apps and networks to build community, rooted in a great home base and supported by a semi-nomadic lifestyle. We will get into some of the nitty-gritty of taxes, insurance and legal domicile and how that fits into decisions about place and travel in the next chapter.

10

The Details: Taxes, Domicile, Mail & Insurance

Up to this point we have covered the rationale and the process of identifying a place and adopting a lifestyle that promotes health, community and freedom. Now we turn attention to the details of setting up a home that supports a semi-nomadic lifestyle.

There are important considerations that come into play in the choice of a location. Different locales may result in very different tax rates, health care options, homeowners insurance costs and other financial factors. Additionally, when adopting a semi-nomadic lifestyle, you may want to consider your choice of legal domicile, and you will need to think through how you will handle postal mail services, health insurance coverage, vehicle registration, voting and banking services.

Let's discuss each of these in turn, starting with everyone's favorite topic: taxes!

Understanding Total Taxation

Living in Texas, I often hear people talk about how great it is that we don't have any State income tax. I constantly hear comparisons to States like California, which has a top State income tax rate of 12.3%, imposed on incomes above $677,276, plus an additional 1% mental health tax imposed on anyone with reported income over $1 million. But Texas has some of the highest property tax rates in the country, averaging 1.8% of the home's assessed value — more than twice California's property tax rates, which in turn are capped under the Proposition 13 rules based on the value at the time the home was purchased. The simple fact is, someone has to pay for the roads, schools and fire and police services, and that money has to come from somewhere. Different States have different methods of raising the money. Texas benefits from taxes imposed on oil and gas pipeline operators, while Florida generates significant revenue from hotel occupancy taxes that are mainly paid by out of state tourists, and Delaware receives the bulk of its money from corporate franchise taxes paid by the millions of Delaware-registered corporations.

Another very important consideration is what kind of income is taxed. In some States, social security payments and distributions from retirement savings programs are considered taxable income, while in other States this money is tax free. And then there is sales tax, levied in all but 5 States (the exceptions being Alaska, Delaware, Montana, New Hampshire and Oregon), and ranging from 2.9% in Colorado to 7.5% in California. In addition to the State-mandated sales tax, many local jurisdictions add an additional amount to the sales tax rate. In California, the average sales tax after local surtaxes is 8.44%. In Colorado, the average sales tax rate is 7.44% and can run as high as 10%, and even in States like Alaska, with no State-mandated sales tax, local jurisdictions like Anchorage impose a 5% sales tax. Sales tax is a consumption tax — it doesn't matter where your income comes from, if you buy things in that State you will pay the tax.

While there are several other types of taxes that may factor into your decision (such as, in particular, an estate or inheritance tax, which 17 States impose), I want to focus on one other tax rate that impacts almost everyone: the gasoline tax. While you might be able to avoid this tax by driving less (or driving an electric vehicle!), it is important to build this into your evaluation of total taxation. Three States in particular stand out for their high gasoline tax rates: California (77.9 cents/gallon), Illinois (66.5 cents) and Pennsylvania (62.2 cents). Alaska has the lowest gas tax, at 8.95 cents per gallon, and in the lower 48, Missouri is the cheapest, at 17.47 cents. The belt of southern States running from Mississippi to Arizona also have relatively low gas tax rates, ranging from 18.4 to 20 cents per gallon.

While I'm not a CPA (although my wife is, but she isn't focused on this kind of tax work), I have prepared a simple guide to help you think through the total taxation that different areas will impose. There are of course many factors that can affect your taxable income, such as mortgage interest deductions and charitable giving. But for simplicity's sake, I've built out a model assuming annual taxable income of $150,000, a home valued at $500,000 (good luck finding that in California!), annual expenses subject to sales tax of $50,000 (at the highest State-authorized tax rate, including local surcharges), and driving 30,000 miles per year in gasoline-powered vehicles averaging 25 miles per gallon (two vehicles per household driven 15,000 miles each). These are round figures designed to show the relative tax hit from living in different areas. I used average property tax and sales tax rates for the State, which of course can vary across different municipalities. The model also assumes all of the sales-taxable expenses and gasoline purchases are made in the State of residence. The income shown here is ordinary, wage and salary income, and is based on a married couple filing jointly, with no dependents. If your income is primarily from retirement plans or Social Security, then that portion may not be taxable in a given State. I used the State tax estimator at www.tax-rates.org, which factors in standard deductions and other exemptions to compute an estimate of the State income tax hit. You can, of course, play with these assumptions, and I'd encourage you to build your own spreadsheet to compute your total tax bill as you consider various residential locations.

Let's look at the results for 6 potential locations: Texas, Florida, Oregon, South Carolina, North Carolina, and Colorado. I chose these because, in part, they are all places with a lot of nice, walkable communities, and are considered prime retirement locales for many people.

		Texas		Florida		Oregon
State income tax on $150,000 taxable income (W2 income, married, filing jointly)	$	-	$	-	$	12,100
Property tax on $500,000 home	$	9,000	$	4,450	$	4,850
Sales tax on $50,000 expenditures	$	4,125	$	3,750	$	-
Gas tax on 30,000 miles per year at 25 MPG	$	240	$	423	$	432
TOTAL TAX	**$**	**13,365**	**$**	**8,623**	**$**	**17,382**

		South Carolina		North Carolina		Colorado
State income tax on $150,000 taxable income (W2 income, married, filing jointly)	$	7,292	$	6,213	$	5,381
Property tax on $500,000 home	$	2,850	$	4,200	$	2,550
Sales tax on $50,000 expenditures	$	4,500	$	3,750	$	5,000
Gas tax on 30,000 miles per year at 25 MPG	$	345	$	489	$	286
TOTAL TAX	**$**	**14,987**	**$**	**14,652**	**$**	**13,217**

While these results cover Statewide averages for just a few potential locations, the results are interesting. Florida emerges as the bargain State, with a total tax hit of just over $8,600. And Texas, despite having no State income tax, winds up imposing a higher tax burden than Colorado, with the latter State's income tax offset by a much lower property tax rate. North and South Carolina trade off in interesting ways, yielding effectively the same tax bill, despite differing approaches to generating income through income, property and sales taxes. And the tax cost of these States is only slightly more than that of Texas and Colorado. Oregon, with its high income tax, despite having no sales tax, has the highest gross tax amount in this comparison, more than double that of Florida.

Once income shifts to Social Security payments, the math changes further. 13 States, including our winner above - Colorado, tax Social Security income. The others are Connecticut, Kansas, Minnesota, Missouri, Montana, Nebraska, New Mexico, North Dakota, Rhode Island, Utah, Vermont, and West Virginia.

Most States tax income derived from 401(k) and IRA account withdrawals (although defined benefit pension plan payments and military retirement payments are not taxed in many States). According to AARP, there are only 13 States that do not count any income from 401(k), IRA or pension plans as part of your taxable income: From east to west, these are New Hampshire, Pennsylvania, Florida, Tennessee, Mississippi, Illinois, Iowa, Texas, South Dakota, Wyoming, Nevada, Washington and Alaska. To further complicate things, Alabama and Hawaii don't tax any pension plan payments, but do tax 401(k) and IRA withdrawals.[21]

So, as you can see, understanding the tax impact of living in a different place depends not only on the types of taxes that are imposed in that State, but also on the type of income you receive.

This is a complicated topic, and a full analysis of the relative tax burden from living in various locations is not only beyond the scope of this book, it is also beyond my ability to advise you. But I trust that the basic framework provided here will help you to consider the variables at work in the decision. Please consult with a qualified tax advisor for a more complete analysis of your choices.

Domicile

While it may seem simple to say that your domicile is where you reside, for those with a nomadic lifestyle, this may be a more complicated question. Domicile and residency are often used as interchangeable terms; but, in fact, they can be different. If you intend to spend a considerable percentage of time living and working remotely, even if you own a home in one location, you may do well to evaluate your choice of domicile carefully. This is explained well in an article on the escapees.com website, "The Ultimate Guide for Residency and Domicile as a Full-Time RVer."[22] A domicile is defined as "the place to where you permanently live and during temporary absences, the place where you intend to permanently return." You have only one domicile, at any given time. Most of us experience this distinction at a few periods of our lives. Living in a college dorm does not mean you have to update your driver's license and voter registration, if your childhood bedroom is ready and waiting any time you want to go home. But if you move permanently and do not clearly establish a new domicile, this can raise several issues:

- Your driver's license, vehicle registration, auto and health insurance coverage may not be valid
- You may not be able to vote where you live
- If you die, your estate may be subject to probate or estate taxes in an old State
- If you are sued, the relevant jurisdiction may also be the State where you previously resided.

In short, while you have only one domicile, you can have countless residences. The Escapees article tells one particularly interesting case study.

> *Back in the early 2000's when George W. Bush was running for president, he asked Dick Cheney to find him a suitable running mate. Cheney looked long and hard for this running mate before deciding the obvious best choice was himself, Dick Cheney. So, George W. Bush announced that Dick Cheney would be his running mate. There was an instant and loud cry of protest. The United States Constitution clearly states that the president and vice president cannot be domiciled in the same state.*
>
> *At that time, George W. Bush was governor of Texas and Dick Cheney ran Halliburton and lived in Dallas, Texas. As soon as the protest began, Dick Cheney announced to*

> *the world, "I am now domiciled in Wyoming!" And, thus, Cheney changed his domicile from Texas to Wyoming. He stated his intent to make it his home. Needless to say, it helped that he already owned a house in Wyoming and had been a Congressman from Wyoming before taking the job with Halliburton in Dallas. For the purpose of being a running mate to George Bush, though, all he needed to do was to state his intent. His staff then helped him make the obvious, but necessary changes so that his vehicles were registered in Wyoming, his drivers license was changed to Wyoming and his voter registration was changed to Wyoming. That's how easy it is when you have residences in several states.*

If you have a residence in more than one State, or if you plan to travel extensively and eventually return to a given State, it may be worthwhile to explore the benefits of setting up your legal domicile in one location over another. A few States make this easy, while many are quite hard. Options that many people like are Texas, Florida and South Dakota, due to a combination of a low tax burden along with services that make it relatively painless to establish domicile, obtain a driver's license and voter registration, and arrange for mail delivery service.

If you are employed and creating a domicile for tax or ultimate destination purposes, you should check with your employer. Quite often, if the corporation does not already have a business presence in a given State, it can be problematic to have a single employee declaring residence in that State. This creates a need for the corporation to register with the relevant State agencies for unemployment insurance payments, business franchise taxes, worker's compensation insurance, and requirements such as disability insurance and sexual harassment awareness and prevention programs that are mandated by some States. During the Covid-19 pandemic, many workers left places like New York and Chicago and worked remotely from their home town or the beach in Florida, and some decided not to return. When their companies found this out, it quite often presented a problem.

Keep in mind that this is a complex issue with significant legal ramifications. Escapees is just one organization that can walk you through the process. You should obtain legal advice before deciding on a domicile that may differ from an address where you primarily reside.

Mail Delivery

Another issue to consider with a semi-nomadic lifestyle is how you will receive your mail. Of course, it is easy to arrange for routine bills and bank statements to be delivered electronically. But there are still some things that arrive courtesy of the US Postal Service. IRS notices are a case in point. Hopefully that isn't something you need to deal with often, but should the IRS need to send any sort of notification, they only communicate by mail. Other important financial documents, such as W2 and 1099 statements, are often mailed. Same with vehicle registration renewal notices, jury duty notices, and those all too frequent notifications that your data has been stolen from some company you dealt with years ago, and now you can sign up for yet another identity protection service. If you are going to be away from your residence for weeks or months at a time, it can be important to receive these materials on a timely basis. Thankfully, there are a variety of services that make this easy for nomads. For between $8 and $30 a month, a service will receive your mail and scan it into an online portal, from where you can elect to have it shredded, opened and scanned, or forwarded to you wherever you might be. Some of these services will even forward mail internationally. A few examples of these services are iPostal1.com, PhyscialAddress.com, and PostScanMail.com. You select from the hundreds of available addresses that these services provide, and then complete USPS Form 1583, which designates the virtual mailbox provider as your agent to receive your mail.

Note that this postal receiving address does not have to be the same address you have set as your domicile. You can register your vehicles, sign up to vote, and assign your insurance coverage to a different address than where you have set your mail to be delivered.

However, if you use a service like Escapees to set up a domicile for you in Texas, Florida or South Dakota, that becomes your "permanent" address. This is where you will visit the local DMV or County tax office to register a vehicle, and where you will be registered to vote. As such, it is important to realize that you will need to visit this location at least once, and possibly as often as once a year, for things like vehicle registration renewals, emissions inspections, and if you want to vote in person.

Insurance

Insurance coverage is also highly variable by location - and this includes home, auto and health insurance plans.

Along with the cost of taxes, homeowners insurance rates also vary tremendously between different areas of the country. This is largely reflective of the risk of damaging storms and disasters in different regions, such as tornadoes, hail and hurricanes. Bankrate.com provides a convenient table of the average homeowner's insurance cost by State[23] based on a $250,000 home, and an indexed score for homeowner's insurance cost is included in the Lifescapes model. The lowest cost for such coverage is in Hawaii, at $382/year. On the mainland, Vermont ($658), Delaware ($679), Utah ($696), New Hampshire ($736) and New Jersey ($775) have relatively low insurance rates. The highest homeowner's insurance costs, by contrast, are in Tornado Alley: Oklahoma ($3,659) and Kansas ($3,083).

Health insurance coverage can vary in price by up to 350% between the least and most expensive States. Data from the Centers for Medicare & Medicaid Services (CMS) provides a synopsis of the average monthly health insurance costs, as well as maximum out-of-pocket costs (MOOP) associated with that coverage. This analysis shows that the least expensive plans are found in Virginia, with average monthly premiums of $431 and MOOP of $6,437. At the other end of the spectrum, New York has the most expensive health insurance, with average monthly premiums of $1,533 and MOOP of $8,558.[24] The popular States for nomad domiciles - Florida, Texas and South Dakota — also have some of the most expensive average health insurance costs.

If you are covered by a corporate-sponsored health insurance plan, as long as the company is OK with you residing in the State of your choice, this is not a problem. But if you are self-employed or retired and not yet covered by Medicare, the cost of insurance can be a significant variable in your personal equation. Bear in mind also that if you are shopping for individual insurance coverage through the ACA Exchange or other private plans, you need to be cognizant of the geographic scope of the plan's network. Some ACA plans provide networks that only cover the State of residence, with coverage outside of this area charged at the higher Out of Network rates.

This again is a broad brush discussion of a complex topic. Please consult with a qualified advisor regarding your health insurance coverage needs.

Other Financial Services

Your choice of a domicile may also impact your relationship with your bank and auto insurance companies. If you do not have a fixed, permanent, physical address, some banks and auto insurers may not be willing to do business with you. Under the Know Your Customer rules for the U.S. banking system, it is incumbent of a financial institution to have accurate information on the physical address of account holders. Auto insurance also is based on where the vehicle is garaged, with some exceptions, for instance, related to a child away at college. If you are nomadic and your address is variable, you may find yourself denied coverage. Furthermore, banks and insurance companies will typically not accept a PO Box or a mail forwarding service address for their customers. The domicile services offered by organizations like Escapees get around this issue, in that they do provide a fixed, permanent, physical address for their members — even if you only visit once, when you first set up the service.

This is a lot of information, and hopefully has enabled you to look at the choice of location and the nitty-gritty of a semi-nomadic lifestyle with a clear perspective on some of the issues you need to consider. But thankfully, you are not alone. Many people have walked this path, and many services exist to take care of the details. A list of the various services covered in this chapter are included in the Appendix to this book.

III

Taking Action

"There are risks and costs to action. But they are far less than the long-range risks of comfortable inaction."
— John F. Kennedy

Hopefully, the data, trends and examples covered in this book have inspired you to make a change in your life. In this final section, we will walk through what's involved in creating your own, personal Lifescapes plan.

11

Are You Ready?

So what's holding you back? Is it time for you to escape the sedentary suburbs, free up equity, and move to a walkable neighborhood with a home base that supports a semi-nomadic lifestyle?

Let's take a look at three scenarios for the impact this could have.

Scenario #1: The Smiths of Naperville, IL - Pre-Retired and Ready to Relocate

Our first hypothetical couple is John & Mary Smith (how's that for some bland, middle-American names; and I apologize if those are the names of any of my readers...) The Smiths live in Naperville, Illinois. They bought a new construction home in 1998 for $565,000 - a hefty sum at the time. As their income improved and interest rates fell, they were able to refinance the remaining balance of $375,000 to a 15 year mortage at 3.6%, and they now owe around $150,000 on the home, with a monthly payment of $2,635. In the meantime, the property value has risen to $1.2 million. They raised two kids in this home, and benefited from being zoned for Naperville North High School, which scores a 10 on the Great Schools ranking. But at this point they are empty-nesters and the kids are finally off the payroll. The 3,850 square foot, 4 bedroom, 3.5 bath home doesn't really serve their needs anymore. Their jobs allow them to work remotely from anywhere, with occasional business travel.

The Smiths decide to relocate to Chattanooga, Tennessee. This mid-sized city with a vibrant downtown and ample access to nature is a welcome change from the Chicago suburbs, not least given the fact that they can get rid of their snow blower. Business travel is facilitated by either flights from Chattanooga itself, or via the shuttle bus that runs several times each day nonstop to the Atlanta airport. They settle on a 2 bedroom, 2.5 bath, 3-story townhome in the Southside Historic District, with a Walkscore of 72. In Naperville, there was not really anything they could walk to from their home. In their new home in Chattanooga, they are walking distance from 2 parks, 6 grocery stores and 26 restaurants. They buy the townhome for $420,000, and pay cash.

Now let's do the numbers (using property tax, homeowners insurance and HOA fee data from Realtor.com for two sample addresses in these areas):

	Naperville	Chattanooga
Mortgage principal and interest	$ 2,635	$ -
Property Tax	$ 1,784	$ 262
Homeowners Insurance	$ 286	$ 217
HOA fee		$ 50
Utilities	$ 500	$ 250
Total Monthly Cost	**$ 5,205**	**$ 779**

By freeing up the equity in their suburban family home and purchasing a smaller "lock and leave" townhouse, they have eliminated their monthly mortgage payment, reduced their property tax bill by 86%, and cut their monthly utility costs in half. They have reduced their monthly expenses by over $4,400. And after paying off the remaining mortgage on the Naperville home and buying the Chattanooga townhouse with cash, they have about $550,000 left over net of the real estate agent commission and moving costs. They put $75,000 of this into the purchase of a used Chevy Silverado 1500 pickup truck and a 27' Forest River Ibex travel trailer. Covered storage for the trailer costs $150/month at a place about 10 miles outside of Chattanooga. In the heat of the summer, when Tennessee can get a little muggy, they can take the trailer up Door County, Wisconsin, where several of their old friends spend time. They are thinking of an even longer "work-cation" swing, covering Theodore Roosevelt National Park, Mount Rushmore and Yellowstone, and swinging back through the Ozarks, with a final stop at Graceland in Memphis, Tennessee. Equipped with a T-Mobile 5G internet device that they can take along on the trip, as long as they have cell coverage, they can keep up with their jobs.

They are also thinking of configuring the townhouse for occasional AirBnB rentals while they are away. They install a deadbolt on an upstairs closet to lock away valuables and install a Google Nest Home monitoring system that can lock doors, view cameras, turn off lights and detect water leaks when they are away. Using data from AirDNA, they determine that their home could command nightly rentals of $200, with an 80% occupancy rate. They consider leaving town during the Chattanooga Motorcar Festival in October, when vintage race cars run a street course through the downtown area. Testing the waters with this in the first year, they are able to take advantage of the IRS' "Master's Rule" — coined by homeowners in Augusta, GA who rent out their homes for the annual Masters Golf Tournament — which makes income from rental of a primary residence tax free as long as it is for less than 15 days per year.

The remaining $475,000 from the sale of their house, after buying the townhome, the truck and the RV, is put into a balanced set of ETFs, which will hopefully gain 8% per year, allowing it to approximately double over the next 10 years until their planned full retirement age. That's a cool million on top of a career of 401(k) plan accumulation.

With one of their children attending graduate school in Madison, Wisconsin, and the other now living in Austin, they have the flexibility to visit them when it is convenient, and the ability to leave their new home base unattended for weeks or months at a time. The financial freedom they have gained from this move opens up a lot of options, not least of which is the choice for at least one of them to fully retire earlier than would have been necessarily if they had remained in Illinois.

Scenario #2: The Johnsons of Austin, TX - Moving Across the Metro Area

Our second couple is George & Karina Johnson, who live in Circle C Ranch southwest of Austin, TX. They bought this house in 2005, in part to be close to a private Christian school that their three kids attended. The youngest has just graduated from Texas A&M (Gig 'em!) on a full tuition scholarship, which was a serious financial blessing as they approached retirement. As they look forward to this next phase of life, the Johnsons are eager to cut back on expenses. Further, George had a scare with non-Hodgkins Lymphoma in his 40s, and while he has been in remission for 15 years, he wants to ensure a healthy lifestyle, with a greater ability to walk for routine errands.

Their 5-bedroom, 4 bathroom, 3,800 square foot home was purchased for $375,000 in 2005. It is now worth $900,000. Taxes are $13,700 per year. They financed with a traditional 30 year mortgage, and now owe less than $100,000 on the home, although they have recently taken a $50,000 HELOC to update the kitchen and master bath and replace the carpeting to get it ready to sell.

The Johnsons would prefer to remain in the Austin metropolitan area, as two of their three children settled locally after college, and they have one grandchild and another on the way. Their oldest daughter attended Southwestern University in Georgetown, Texas and they really like that area. Furthermore, since their son and daughter-in-law now live in Round Rock, Texas, being on the northern side of the metro area makes more sense to them than Circle C.

They find a 2 bedroom, 2 bath condo in Georgetown overlooking the San Gabriel river and walking distance to the attractive downtown square. While the HEB supermarket is a short drive away, the weekly Farmer's Market is 4/10th of a mile walk, and there are 46 restaurants, bars and coffee shops within a one mile radius. The neighborhood Walkscore is 83. At $600,000, this unit is priced at the top of what they can afford without having to take out a mortgage, but it offers a quality of life and scenic beauty that checks all the boxes for them. And it puts them less than 30 minutes away from the grandchildren.

So how do the numbers work out for the Johnsons?

	Circle C Ranch	Georgetown
Mortgage principal and interest (including HELOC)	$ 2,475	$ -
Property tax	$ 1,143	$ 603
Homeowners insurance	$ 697	$ 440
HOA fee	$ 68	$ 499
Utilities	$ 500	$ 175
Total Monthly Cost	**$ 4,883**	**$ 1,717**

While the Georgetown condo has a much higher monthly HOA expense (due to the condominium covering all exterior maintenance, roof, community facilities and security), the tax bill is cut almost in half, and the energy efficiency of a unit with shared walls results in substantially lower utility costs. Eliminating a mortgage of course has the greatest impact. The Johnsons recognize a monthly savings of $3,166 from downsizing. Coupled with a more walkable environment and proximity to grandchildren, they are well positioned for a healthier and happier context for their early retirement years.

Scenario #3 - The Wardzynskis of Detroit, MI - Trying out Van Life

Now we will take a look at a younger couple, Joe and Cynthia Wardzynski of Southfield, Michigan. This couple is in their late 20s. They have been married only two years and do not yet have any children — although that might be on the horizon in a few years. This is different from the typical Lifescapes model, in that this young couple do not have significant home equity to cash in. But let's see what could make sense for them.

Joe and Cynthia have been renting an apartment in Southfield, at $1,700/month. Joe works in an ad agency serving the automotive industry, and Cynthia is a nurse. Joe's job allows him to work remotely and Cynthia is considering a transition to either Travel Nursing or medical case review. While they both grew up in the Detroit area, they are eager for a warmer climate, as well as for the freedom to travel America.

They decide on a somewhat radical next step. They have saved up for the down payment on a home, but have decided to establish a home base that can also be AirBnB'd, allowing them to travel semi-nomadically. Joe bought a used conversion van and has renovated it in his spare time. The 22' van has a fold-down bed, a kitchenette, and a "wet bath" at the back. They plan to travel at least six months of the year, going further south in the winter and joining friends who have a lake house near Traverse City, Michigan in the warm summer months.

For their home base, they settle on Raleigh, NC. Joe's firm has an office that allows his employment domicile to be established in North Carolina, and the area offers a lot of future opportunities should they decide to get off the road. They find a 2 bed, 2 bath, 1,158 square foot condo in downtown Raleigh for $440,000, which is at the top end of what they can qualify for with the $50,000 down payment they have managed to save. They hope to put another $35,000 into the principal of the home in the next year or two to eliminate the PMI expense. Using AirDNA, they estimate that they can achieve a $195/night rent when they are away, with a 65% occupancy rate. This should generate approximately $22,000 in annual income, with about $5,000 in expenses for cleaning and maintenance.

This condo is in a Walker's Paradise, with a Walk Score of 96, as well as having fairly good transit options. A grocery store is next door and there are over 50 food and drink establishments within a few blocks. The local high school, Needham Broughton, located just 3/10th of a mile away, registers a 7 out of 10 on the Great Schools scale. It has a college readiness score of 10 out of 10, meaning that this school is well above the state average in key measures of college and career readiness, such as graduation rates, college entrance exams, and advanced courses.

The math here is quite different from our earlier examples, but nonetheless encouraging. While housing in Raleigh is more expensive than in the suburbs of Detroit, and the Wardzynskis are taking on a significant expense with the mortgage, property taxes and condo fees, on net their monthly expenses only increase by $590. Plus they have the freedom to explore all that Van Life has to offer.

	Southfield	Raleigh
Rent	$ 1,700	
Mortgage principal and interest		$ 2,910
Property tax		$ 352
Homeowners / renters insurance	$ 100	$ 172
HOA fee		$ 448
Utilities	$ 200	$ 125
Total Monthly Cost	**$ 2,000**	**$ 4,007**
AirBnB income		$ 1,417
Net Monthly Cost	**$ 2,000**	**$ 2,590**

This model assumes a 10% down payment and an 8% interest rate on a 30-year mortgage. If they are able to increase the equity share to 20% of the value of their home (perhaps with a one-time gift from one of their parents), they could reduce the mortgage payment by several hundred dollars. Nonetheless, this is a relatively affordable housing option for a young couple with two good jobs.

But importantly, in this scenario, the Wardzynskis are building equity, along with the flexibility and future prospects that the condo in Raleigh creates for them. Over time, if they decided to operate this unit as a short-term rental permanently, it could potentially be cash flow neutral, while continuing to appreciate in value. As part of a longer-term strategy for wealth creation, it is a good first step.

Your Turn

These examples illustrate the premise of Lifescapes in action. The core audience for this book is the millions of Americans who have gained significant equity in a suburban home that is no longer appropriate to their needs. But there are many permutations for how this model could work for you, and the basic idea of minimizing housing costs and choosing to reside in a walkable neighborhood that enables a semi-nomadic lifestyle can work for anyone, at any age.

To build your own Lifescape, you need to consider:

- Is the place you live now suited to your needs?
- Could the equity be better deployed by downsizing and relocating?
- What specific neighborhoods are best aligned to your priorities?
- How do you want to organize your life to allow for the greatest geographic flexibility?

The Low-Cost Probe

Before you move half-way across the country and make a radical change to your living arrangements, I would advise you to make some low-cost probes.

Consider a couple of potential locations. The neighborhood search tool at model.lifescapes.info provides a great means of pinpointing your best options. Think about what is important in a locale, and whether you know people or have other relationships that could help to ease the transition. Rent an AirBnB in your target neighborhoods — preferably over both a weekend and week days, so that you get a feel for the rhythm of the place. Strike up conversations with people in a coffee shop or walking their dogs in a park, to find out what they like (and dislike) about the area. Visit a local church. If you see a police officer on the street, ask him or her what crime is like in the area. Do all this before you talk to a real estate agent. Their job is to sell you a house, and they are proscribed by the regulations of their industry to not be able to discuss some aspects of a location that might be important to you.

In my view, it is worthwhile to spend several months to a year on this process, exploring several potential areas. While you might have a specific need or desire to settle in one specific locale, I think it is best to keep an open mind as long as possible. The low-cost probe can save you from a decision you might later regret.

Your Lifescapes Resources

Lifescapes stands ready to assist you in this process. In the Appendix to this book, you will find a listing a several resources that have been discussed in these pages, with links to their websites and referral codes for some of the services.

The neighborhood search tool at model.lifescapes.info provides a great way to search for ideal locations across the country that meet your needs. Using the SMARTER scoring methodology, the website enables you to set baseline measures, and then drag and drop your criteria in the rank order of their importance to you. Once you create a user account on the Lifescapes website, you are able to enter any number of decision criteria and save the results, allowing you to explore many different options.

We also stand ready to assist you in your journey. You can book a complimentary, 30-minute consultation with a Lifecapes coach to discuss your priorities for finding a place and living your dream. Then, if you are interested, we can map out a process to assist you along the journey, including connecting you with financial, legal and real estate professionals to provide the specific services you may need.

Your path to a rewarding Lifescape awaits. As JFK once said, "there are risks and costs to action. But they are far less than the long-range risks of comfortable inaction." Are you ready to take the first step? I hope you are, and I welcome the opportunity to hear from you as to how it works out. You can send me a note through the lifescapes.info website, or email me at drbarber@lifescapes.info.

Onward to a happier, healthier and more rewarding tomorrow!

12

Appendix: Resources for Your Lifescape

Hopefully this book has stirred you to action. As you work through the process of finding your place and living your dream, here are a few helpful resources.

Lifescapes.info

Our website contains a free tool, the Lifescapes Model, which allows you to search and identify walkable communities based on your own customized decision criteria. Once you create a user account, you can run as many searches as you want and save the results for future reference. Additional functionality will be added to the site in the future, including links to local real estate profiles and listings. You can also book a free, 30 minute consultation to see if any of our private or group coaching services could be helpful to you.

Escapees.com

This organization offers an array of support services specifically tailored to people living long-term on the road. This includes assistance with creating a domicile, mail forwarding services, discounts on gear, and a wide range of community-building programs.

```
Use this affiliate link:
https://www.escapees.com/refer/Lifescapes
```

Remoteyear.com

Remote Year brings together remote workers and digital nomads as a community to work and explore in 80+ destinations around the world, one month at a time. Working remotely and traveling solo can be daunting, time-consuming, and isolating, so let Remote Year take care of the planning for you. Now, with more flexible and affordable options than ever, Remote Year has a program for every type of remote professional, budget, and lifestyle.

```
Use this affiliate link:
https://www.remoteyear.com/?ref=njq3ytd
```

Data Resources to Evaluate Locations

As you consider relocation, there are several resources beyond what is available on lifescapes.info that you may want to explore for more detailed information.

walkscore.com

Data on walkability for any street address in America

greatschools.org

A 1-10 rating for almost every school in America

crimegrade.org

A heatmap display with a letter grade for relative crime rates for every ZIP code

bankrate.com

Provides a cost of living comparison calculator and other financial tools

airdna.co

Calculates the AirBnB rental potential for any address

tax-rates.org

Shows County-level property tax rates as well as a calculator for State income tax

Domiciliary and Mail Forwarding Services

In addition to the permanent legal domicile and mail forwarding service offered by Escapees (and several other organizations), it is also possible to just utilize an agent to receive and process your mail. If you plan to live semi-nomadically, it can make a lot of sense to set this up ahead of time, so you no longer have to worry about creating a mail hold every time you are away. This avoid sthe risk of not receiving an important notice on a timely basis.

A few options for mail forwarding services, where you can choose between addresses in many different cities and States, are listed here.

ipostal1.com
physicaladdress.com
postscanmail.com
travelingmailbox.com

Notes

REALITY 2023

1 Based on data tracked by Realtor.com. For a summary of the trends, see: https://www.forbes.com/advisor/mortgages/median-home-prices-increase/

2 The rate of working from home is tracked monthly by researchers at Stanford University's Institute for Economic Policy Research. For a summary of their research, see Barrero, Jose Maria, Nicholas Bloom, and Steven J. Davis, 2021. "Why working from home will stick," National Bureau of Economic Research Working Paper 28731.

3 From 1980 to 2019, the incidence rate of working from home was tracked as part of the U.S. Census Bureau's American Community Survey. It was initially 0.6% of American workers in 1980, reaching 4.7% in January, 2019 before exploding during the Covid-19 pandemic.

4 These statistics come from a variety of sources, and are summarized on *The Ultimate List of Remote Work Statistics: The 2023 Edition*. http://smallbizgenius.net/by-the-numbers/remote-work-statistics/

5 https://www.businessofapps.com/data/microsoft-teams-statistics/

6 https://windowsreport.com/most-us-companies-use-microsoft-teams/

7 https://www.investopedia.com/average-equity-in-u-s-homes-5270147

8 https://todayshomeowner.com/blog/guides/cities-most-million-dollar-homes/

9 https://todayshomeowner.com/blog/guides/cities-most-million-dollar-homes/

THE TRUE COST OF HOME OWNERSHIP

10 https://www.bankrate.com/real-estate/property-tax-by-state/

PLACE IS THE PROBLEM ... AND THE SOLUTION

11 Vivek Murthy, "Work and the Loneliness Epidemic," *Harvard Business Review*, September 26, 2017.

LOCK, LEAVE, LOVE

12 MBO Partners, 2022. "Working from the Road: The Aspirations and Reality for Digital Nomads." Downloaded from https://info.mbopartners.com/rs/mbo/images/2022_Digital_Nomads_Report.pdf

13 https://hbr.org/2012/10/the-truth-behind-the-4-hour-fa

14 There are several stories regarding burn-out among Ferris' virtual assistants. One can be found here: https://medium.com/swlh/tim-ferrisss-assistant-s-sudden-resignation-serves-as-a-warning-for-trying-to-have-it-all-288003e67030

15 Becker, Deanna, June 4, 2018. "'Lock-and-Leave': Low-Maintenance Housing for Active Homeowners." Retrieved from https://www.neighborhoods.com/blog/lock-and-leave-low-maintenance-housing-for-active-homeowners.

THERE'S NO PLACE LIKE HOME

16 The SMARTER method was originally described by Edwards and Barron in a 1994 paper published in the journal *Organizational Behavior and Human Decision Processes* (vol. 60, 306-325).

COMMUNITY

17 The full Public Health Advisory is available at https://www.hhs.gov/sites/default/files/surgeon-general-social-connection-advisory.pdf

18 https://www.forbes.com/sites/tracybrower/2020/10/25/how-to-build-community-and-why-it-matters-so-much/?sh=269971d9751b

19 Kumar, A., & Epley, N. (2021). It's surprisingly nice to hear you: Misunderstanding the impact of communication media can lead to suboptimal choices of how to connect with others. *Journal of Experimental Psychology: General, 150*(3), 595–607. https://doi.org/10.1037/xge0000962

20 *American Journal of Public Health*, 2003 September; 93(9): 1546–1551. https://www.ncbi.nlm.nih.gov/pmc/articles/PMC1448008/#

THE DETAILS: TAXES, DOMICILE, MAIL & INSURANCE

21 https://www.aarp.org/money/taxes/info-2023/states-that-do-not-tax-your-retirement-distributions.html

22 https://escapees.com/establishing-domicile-for-rvers/

23 https://www.bankrate.com/insurance/homeowners-insurance/states/#home-insurance-rates-by-state

24 https://www.moneygeek.com/insurance/health/analysis/health-insurance-costs-state/2023-top-51/

Made in the USA
Monee, IL
04 November 2026

67385500R00066